Business Sparring Logistics

An analysis behind the scenes of logistics management in Germany

About the author and editor:

Roger Heidmann is a trained sea freight inspector and a graduate industrial engineer for transport and logistics. He is managing director and founder of the LSA Logistik Service Agentur GmbH.

LSA has been developing and planning logistics concepts and strategies since 2004. In the form of a think tank, the LSA develops new ideas and concepts for companies from industry, trade and the service sector.

1st edition, 2019

© Roger Heidmann - all rights reserved.

Borgfelder Deich 17, 28357 Bremen

www.logistik-service-agentur.com

It is pointed out that all information and recommendations in this work, despite careful editing, are provided without guarantee and that the author and publisher cannot be held liable.

Table of Content

Prologe

Oblique sketches: Logistics repeats itself, projects are unique, digitization seems abstract.

She fights wars. Travels with coffee, cigarettes, Playmobil and grass. She is influencer: In a tenancy changeover, meddles in everyday life and when business is not going well. She lurks behind doors, in the fog and sends packages into the nirvana. The logistics.

She is often loved - like a home moving. Tiresome to pack. Intolerable circumstances. Transports are stalled: Like a wardrobe that gets stuck in the stairwell. We have preferred nothing to do with her!

But without her we can't do it either. Every time something is missing: parts in production, coffee and cigarettes or the profit in the balance sheet. How do you become better friends? The logistics and you? With more understanding, more trust and a view behind the scenes?

We try headlines, for the discourse! It illuminates new recipes and old trails. We're looking for the explosive and hope that's brings our conversation to life. Combined with the hope that new findings will not only exist in the "cloud".

At the heart of the matter is the question: How do we add a fresh spice to logistics concepts? Like the street food at the festival. With more ingredients, like mint and pepper, instead of flour and sauce thickener? As we know, if too much ends up in the same pot, it spins around more slowly. Water extinguishes, accelerates and has a calming effect. Until you overdo it and whitewash it to the point of taste. Sauce thickeners and flour stick together, just like shipping manager and forwarding agents. Pepper and mint inspire, like project and logistics?

To be honest, at the beginning it was a short publication. An essay on project logistics was requested. In the end, I continued writing. Just go for it. Without knowing exactly where the journey is going. A risk, sure! Just as logistics often is in projects. But don't worry. It is by no means followed by a doctoral thesis or a new non-fiction book - for the shelf. My writing style waived the "scientific correctness" of many fonts. I try to use more a belletristic form.

As in real life, people are the focus of my attention. The protagonists of the story: Larissa, Ethan, Peter and colleagues work on our behalf. They live in the area of conflict between project and logistics. They sound out which perspective achieves the greatest benefit. Learn how the logistics market ticks. You may be surprised how compatible the methods of logistics and project management are. Gain new perspectives and ways, look behind the curtains, view cases and examples. And finally, design your choreographies so that logistics and projects work in harmony.

When the journalist asked me if I like to write an essay on project logistics, I answered spontaneously: "Yes, why not?" So, the drama took its course. My first question was: "What is project logistics anyway?" Sure, I have known the term for almost forty years. Nevertheless, I always start to think anew. "Event logistics" could be used as a technical term or somewhat more unwieldy: "Campaign-based supply chain management". Word combinations that are symptomatic of the wide range of logistics terms. Which ones do you use when you tackle new tasks and projects as a managing director, project manager, logistics manager or forwarder?

And project cargo? Is it only the cargo that do not belong in containers or packages? But what are projects without the boxes? Not the slightest! At least, they provide standardized images. My photos of the project logistics are all unique. Comparison is impossible. However, they shape ideas. For ship owners and ports is the project especially one: Cargo.

The wide range of terms used to describe logistics makes it difficult to draw boundaries. The quickest way to find logistics in the project organization chart is often the "Transport" box. It seems tempting to see logistics through the glasses of transport alone. Together with warehousing and handling, the freight forwarder calls it project logistics

Just for contrast:

Strange pictures - what does an open-air concert have to do with the erection of wind turbines?

"When was the last time you went to an event?"

Say in a concert. Did the orchestra play in unison? Just because of the successful transports? Or about the signals that the conductor transmitted by baton. Was it an open-air concert? In this case the project manager had to deal with the weather additionally.

The same applies to the installation of wind turbines. A similar situation exists in agriculture. The harvest is seasonal and therefore dependent on the weather. What's similar? Looking beyond the horizon allows a simple thesis: Just like the weather, campaigns, events and projects always have an effect along the entire supply chain. Even if it only storms or snows in one place.

It is always the case: The shipment belongs into the right place like the football into the goal. A definition of logistics says eight times "R" for "right": That's the art,

- the right component
- with the right packaging
- at the right time,
- in the right quality
- in the right place
- in the right quantity
- at the right cost
- with the right information
- to be provided.

The right time in football is between the kick-off and the final whistle. The correct quality is the approved football. Only the one ball is the correct quantity. The real customer here, however, is the opponent waiting in the right place, in front of the goal line. The costs are usually fixed for goal celebrations. The appropriate packaging here is rather the unpackaged. The referee's whistle sends the correct information. Transports, in this case passes and flanks, are important, but only intermediate steps. Admittedly, this is an odd comparison with logistics; like so many others.

Optimal is, if gates and transports are avoided. Shippers and consignees usually do not earn their money with it. For them the optimal transport is the one that is avoided. A way of thinking that goes against the grain for most of the transport industry. They work for the utilization of their trucks, ships and trains.

As a result, the view on logistics is different. Everybody plays to win. Accordingly, the strategy is best determined before the game. Chess Grand Master Savielly Tartakower says, "Strategy is knowing what to do; when there is nothing to do." According to this, it would be like finishing chess or football beforehand. Long before the dispatch manager starts the transport.

Another topic reveals additional experiences: The lives of others? How have people fared in projects such as the Elbe Philharmonic or Berlin Airport? Have they drifted in a similar way as to the German offshore wind projects? A glance at the newspaper produced these horrible thoughts. Are your own projects and experiences suitable for comparison? Probably communication flops with many and thus forms the common denominator. Or is it due to the quality of the staff? A logistics manager said, slightly disillusioned, "I can only dance with the daughters who are in the hall."

Help comes might be from the communication and information technology. Their new code name digitalization sends out abstract signals: terms such as "digital transformation", "platform economy" or "new work" appear nebulous. Under the radar it probably provides three things: the chance to automate the flow of information. Gathering experience and knowledge. Leaving old trails and put stumbling blocks aside.

Perhaps a new picture fits in with this: it emerged at the beginning of October. In the area of the Chesapeake Bay, we would say, it´s Indian summer. However, we stayed in the bay area of San Francisco. The first appointment was behind us. The second breakfast was waiting for us. The short path leads across the sun-drenched streets of Palo Alto. We stopped in front of a wonderfully restored historical hall, the company's own restaurant. There, the feeling was like in many corners of the "Bay Area", the special spirit vibrated. It is precisely the founding spirit that so many companies on the left and right of the highway from San Francisco to San Jose radiate.

The presentations impressively substantiate the origin and the trigger of this start up. It is precisely the security of payment transactions on the Internet. The business purpose to save them. Big Data is the master of conversation. The images of impressive dashboards and data analysis remain in your head. I saw a real factory for analyzing data and producing decisions. The answer to my last question before the farewell echoes to this day!

Abstruse question: "What do you actually do when you have no data?"

"Then we're out," was the succinct answer.

My topic: deciding without data has not been solved in my head so far. Big Data flies high, no question. Unfortunately, first-time projects and unique specimens usually leave more white spots on the data map than many people would like. Make decisions without data and in real time is a challenge. Where do we get knowledge from experience that is generally not learnable? The latter demands time, mistakes, work and bankruptcies, only to take a seat in consciousness afterwards.

Artificial intelligence (AI) appears to be a real opportunity in the sense of the well-known expert systems. If only in order to preserve the empirical knowledge of today's older workers in the face of demographic change. By the way, I'm retiring in 2030, so I'm going to start writing; just a few memos like this one.

But let's get back to the topic: "e-commerce", city logistics, 3D printing, "Blockchain" & Co. appear as further drivers on the scene now. If they thrive to a hindrance like safety shoes for new work, then we create time waster considering the topics above. This can be recognized, if the people spoke in possibilities and without solutions. Furthermore, if jurisdictions to be pulled into the field. Opinions are diluted. And the discourse remains outside of the door.

Logistics experts who have the discourse in their blood are probably the best discussion partners for innovative drivers. They do not chat about possibilities but evaluate the solution. They know how to use the new drivers and their capabilities. They have learned that the classic answers alone are no longer enough: For the selection of transport equipment, packaging, service providers or for transport and handling instructions. They know that they are not always brought on board: because there are many roles and even more professional groups in the project boat.

Speaking of boats, let me give you another example of the eternal game between effectiveness and efficiency. Many people try it again and again: sailing directly against the wind. As before, it is doomed to failure. The straighter you sail against the wind the slower boat will be. You end up with flapping sails. Possibly with drifting backwards. Otherwise, the further you drop away from the wind direction, the boat will be gain speed. Just as rapidly one moves away from the goal.

At this point a second quotation of the mentioned chess grandmaster is to be added. He said, "Tactics is knowing what to do when there's something to do." In this case, it means doing the right things effectively and reaching the goal at the best possible time. Efficiency, doing things right means, sailing the boat as fast as possible on the given course. If the course is set incorrectly, you will efficiently and quickly travel in the wrong direction. So, the only question is, at what point it´s going to be wrong?

Okay, in the current project the future comes too late for Larissa, Ethan and Peter. They're sitting on their islands of responsibilities. Furthermore, they fight for the last ten percent of the contract sum, play against time and defy the claims. Islands are logistically expensive. At the end of the day, the baton often falls still yet. Painful examples are the missing permits for oversized and heavy goods transports. In these case Logistics managers find themselves often alone in the corridor.

At this point a first tip with the aim of avoiding sleepless nights and stopovers. Let's be honest: At least the Paragraph 29 transport permit, which in the German Road Traffic Act applies to excessive road use in large-capacity and heavy goods traffic; does it not belong in the hands of the shippers? He knows the data at an early stage, at the latest in engineering department. His purchasing department needs them too, just to request the transport.

Won't there be less sleepless nights if procedures such as preliminary building applications are allowed? The approval becomes more tangible. Only on the day of the start, the contracted transport operator asks the authorities for the starting signal. Further on, it´s thinkable that digital solutions are working in this matter, like the reference judgements in court? Figuratively speaking, these show the routes for transports and routes that have already been approved before.

The example shows the motivation for discourse. This is basically meant as a back and forth conversation. Question and answer, reproach and justification alternate. If we are reading, naturally the own thoughts remain at home alone. Unless what you read prompts you to engage in dialogue. With me, your colleagues, friends, in discussion groups and workshops.

Larissa, Ethan and Peter sometimes represent the discourse. They work for our purposes at a fictitious company. We call it Virtual.AN GmbH & Co KG. 550 employees plan and produce special machines and plants. They achieve an annual turnover of 150 million euros.

The "Inspiration" project provides the impetus. This is the first contract in which the company acts as general contractor. Virtuell.AN is responsible for the complete plant, including the construction of the real estate. A project company was founded specifically for this purpose.

Managing director of both companies is Peter, in his mid-fifties. He studied mechanical engineering, thirty years before. Otherwise, his resume resembles a rollercoaster ride. He is open to new methods. However, he sees parts of his team that don't pursue this always. On weekends he likes sailing, in former times regattas, today with his family. The example of sailing against the wind, with the different between strategy and tactics; he has devised it himself.

Ethan has been hired as project manager. With his 35 years of age he already brings a lot of experience in project management on the table. Ethan is a manager through and through. However, it shows a weakness. Logistics, it's not his favorite subject. Ethan tends to think without them or when it's inevitable. For this reason, Peter brings Larissa on board. She had recently launched her own startup. Virtuell.AN is her first client. Larissa is in her early thirties. Before and after her studies in logistics management and engineering, she worked in large logistics companies and international projects.

Spotlights describes the topics and experiences of the three personalities in the project. According to that a consecutive novel or plot strand for the project or logistics management will be avoided. Rather the three protagonists and the author are happy when new keywords and perspectives for your own projects become apparent. Parallels with living companies, projects or persons are therefore purely coincidental and not intended.

Act One

How do you design the start? By jumping in at the deep end or with methods like SCOR, NWA or Incoterms?

Larissa was keen on the job. She was tingling when her ideas began to take effect. A sure sign for an attractive task.

As always, reality looks different. Months go by. Larissa's first meeting with Peter was in February. At the beginning of December of the same year the kick-off meeting with the project manager Ethan followed. The first relevant information's were available at the end of January. At the meeting almost a year ago, the managing director was open-minded about new approaches in logistics. The buyer and the dispatch manager were also at the table. They speak in the familiar metaphors of transport. See the logistician as a freight forwarder and in competition with her well-known ones.

The first conversation was one in the art of subjunctives. Although the order was already in the house. Larissa briefly hoped that a logistics concept and its cost calculation had been included in the offer. The wealth of variations in the conversation made their hopes fade. In the stars were: the number of delivery locations, the design of components, time schedules and contracts with suppliers.

One year later, a white sheet of paper serves as her starting position. Larissa's tingle is gone. Disillusionment moves in. The blank white an alarm signal! A concept is until missing. In the best case there is a chance for a free development. However, it is more likely that she is standing with her back to the wall from the beginning.

It's like cooking without a recipe. In addition, the view into the pantry shows what is there and what is missing. The menu also includes the inventory. After this appeal following often listless glances in projects. One expects solutions like from the fast food restaurant or the pressure cooker.

The construction site quickly becomes a pressure cooker here. In their case it´s behind a mountain range and 100 km far away from the nearest seaport. The pantry - the warehouse - is filled by providers. They can be found all over Europe. So that Larissa's head created a kind of knitting pattern bow. She starts with the design of the logistics network.

Simple tools like the Supply Chain Reference Model helps. They show each actor where one is active and provide orientation in discussions.

The model provides for four levels. The first level outlines scope and content. It works process-oriented in the categories plan, source, make, deliver and return. Each actor receives its core processes. Source, make, deliver, for example. Means that a supplier is responsible for procurement, production and delivery. If he only receives a make, the line for procurement and delivery necessarily leads to the predecessor and successor. Otherwise, gaps in the system will occur. In any case, the network becomes visibility. At the end, you hold the first draft of the process map in your hand.

On the second level, the network will used to create the project supply chain. The essential processes in the categories are described in more detail. Questions are to be answered: Who delivers something and whereto? Where will produced something? Who deliver to the construction site?

The logistics strategy of the company's also becomes apparent. From the dispatch manager hears Larissa again and again: "That's what our forwarding agent does". In the office of the chief buyer she hears the classical case: "However, you have to ship it for that price to the construction site ". A clear strategic decision: Purchasing and Dispatching keeps the logistics at bay.

In such a case the whole thing is already off the table on level two. The third level would be obsolete! However, details are needed here. For example: It must be clarified where the logistics are procured - regionally or internationally. Key figures or best practices are determined here, without which a later comparison of offers and solutions fails.

Only on the fourth level tasks are developed. Comparisons with the actual situation show the need for new things. The general terms and conditions of every company offer suitable examples. Larissa remembers a previous project: A customer of her previous employer behaved like the buyer of Virtuell.AN. He ordered according to the motto: "For the high price you are also responsible for the transport". Accordingly, they fetched who is the cheapest and he delivered whenever it suited at the best for him. With the result, the inventories increased gradually in their own company. Her employer subsequently buys more parts, as a precaution. The production was pleased with the buffer and they scooped from the full. Employees, who had actually reduced her overtime, installed as long as stocks last. The balance sheet of the company filled up in step with their stock in the warehouse. Until the alarm bells were ringing in Controlling. They turned off the expensive luxury and picked up consignments in her own responsibility. The coordination of resources returned to its own hands. The higher effort for coordination paid off through lower inventories and less storage space.

Tasks and processes are usually only rudimentarily known in the early stages of projects. Nevertheless, one wishes for more than the white leaves, Larissa thinks. She's part of the project team now. Her most urgent task is to derive a logistics plan from the project plan. Frown was the reaction as they asked her what she plans to do first. "Read the contracts," she replies. The documents came only after Peter was asked.

The project plan is often part of the contract. Larissa doesn't read it from the perspective of a lawyer, she uses the logistics glasses. Her focus lays onto the consequences that the contract has for the flow of information and material. For example, some steps, such as setting up the construction site, were completed. Others, such as measurements in the ground, must perform by both partners. The latter passage leads to the conclusion that there have open points on the agreement agenda. With respect to her tasks the positions of the cranes and vehicles to be procured depend on the stability of the ground.

She stumbles about another connection: At the same time as the inspection of the land will done, bank guarantees must be presented; for the transport and lifting equipment. The cranes at which they will the equipment be suspended later, is depending on the load capacity of the ground. Larissa investigates the contract which requirements are described there, without success. Not even the default values for roads and bridges are set. She hears the argument already when the subject is on the table: "Why don't you move the cranes further away, there the ground is stable! This means significantly larger and more expensive cranes. Most of the time, the whole thing becomes a part of a carousel. On the way in each panel, but without a solution afterwards. Until it stopped by events and a contingency plan was in place.

Another question remains open: Are tools, the lifting equipment, the transport frames or both? Hopefully there will be a specification when this point has already been included in the contract and in the project financing. Larissa must check it. A list with all tools, which leads to the last shackle, will find its way onto the "to-do list".

Meanwhile, the contract brings further surprises: Only after the measurements on the construction site the release of the contract can be expected. Okay, thinks Larissa. The deal is not fixed until know. As always, these is a real dilemma: If they are waiting for signatures, there is no time to catch up open tasks. An early start means working at your own risk. As a result, one is stingy with the money for planning. The chances of gaps in the process increase.

Larissa continues to browse on the pages of procurement. The suppliers' payment plans lead to new insights. Already, 65 percent of the contract amount is due with the second invoice. To be paid when the lots are available at the installation site. The question where exactly the point of availability is to be found remains open.

Larissa paints a matrix of the delivery conditions. Many are familiar with the colorful illustrations and the rules between sender and recipient. The cryptic clauses, such as "CIF", "FOB" or "DAP" are recognized worldwide.

Larissa's favorite is the "DAP" case. It's already giving her a headache. He is characterized by the fact that the supplier makes his consignment available at the specified location. The unloading as well as the costs and risks belong to the project. The more uncertain the place and time, the higher the effort for the project.

She suspects that the designers of the contracts wanted the ideal: in principle to be mounted directly from the truck. Like a concrete mixer for pour foundations. This can be told comfortably and vividly at the green table. At the end only the address remains in the contract. The correct installation location is missing in the drawings. Again, an expensive loophole in the details.

Incoterms like "DAP", are for Larissa blessing and curse. They help to clarify the interfaces, which is good! Unless you stop too soon, as in the previous example. The filling of the gap is then quickly a painful one, just as a toothache leads to the dentist. It becomes a curse if functional thinking in responsibility prevails there. Imagine the dentist remains sitting with crossed arms on his chair. If you´re sitting on his treatment chair headfirst, because the delivery conditions for the next injections are unclear. Do the "Incoterms" encourage such kind of thinking?

Larissa's assignment had nothing to do with Incoterms. She only remembers how it came about. Months after the initial interview, she receives a call for tender from Virtuell.AN. This showed well how thinking in delimited functions works. Logistics was conveniently equated here with freight forwarding. The wish of the chief buyer prevailed. Efforts were made to put a package of the gaps in the logistics system together and to assign it to a forwarding agent.

The hope was quickly evaporated for a quick comparison of the offers. She was told afterwards, about that episode. The offers all presented more exclusions than contents. Therefore, more gaps appeared.

The carriers replied in line with their own objectives. These means: Utilize your own assets first. The best provider suggested to set up a central warehouse in his branch office 60 kilometers away. The construction site should be supplied from there. This seemed logical for the purchasing department at first. Especially as there were more important issues on the table than the remaining logistics tasks.

When Larissa was confronted with this solution, she asked: Why do you define structures before you have fixed processes? She illustrated the question with an example: At the beginning there are two information channels between customer and project. If you include material and cash flows, six compounds are obtained. Adding the first supplier the numbers triples from six to 18. The fourth element increases it six-fold to 36 and so on. Beyond a detailed analysis; how can you conclude that the best solution is a central warehouse 60 kilometers away? Whoever is right about this becomes a clairvoyant and is better off in other industries. Larissa cultivated the doubts.

Irritation and annoyance alternated in purchasing. Three comparable offers, nil. The basis for negotiating prices, none. It's hard to make an expert opinion. The reasoning for the order, at most inaccurate!

In the meanwhile, Larissa cancelled Peter and Virtuell.AN. She had no warehouse to offer, exactly 60 kilometers away from the construction site. With her cancellation, the hanging game gained a momentum. Peter asked in the purchase department: "What was going on?" Added to this was pressure from the customer. He was suddenly interested in carrying out the logistics himself. He made the same offer. However, he put a lot of salt in the soup. They demanded the reduction of the order amount. 20

percent of 50 million euros was suddenly in the room. A price reduction through the back door? Or, was that the evaluated benefit for logistics? Peter found the number alarmingly high. The question that needs to be clarified becomes obvious:

Which view on logistics achieves the greatest benefit? The good old cost-benefit analysis helps.

The price reduction is substantially. The customer has setting probably itself into his head to make money with it. In Peters own house, purchasing and shipping are pushing for the "buy" to get things off the table. Larissa's proposal provides for a well-tempered mix. She's pursuing a hybrid solution.

There are three possible ways: "make", "buy" or "hybrid"? For Peter is the decision like driving a car without a navigation system and without knowing the place. If you turn the wrong way and don't turn back: We hope it gets better before it gets worse. In contrast to that, a turnaround costs time immediately. The error becomes visible for everyone.

Hybrid is a kind of in between. Is without doubt modern. Everywhere, where we are shape a new whole from two different origins. But how does that work in logistics? The constantly remixing of alliances, technologies and traditional means is daily business. Larissa sees the logistician as intermediary. He creates new dynamics, like the switching game in soccer. For this he needs scope of action.

But how is the scope of action to be laid? The engineers at Virtuell.AN work a lot in calculation, the styling of constructions, the measure of components or the check of welding seams. In the end they keep their promises. In such kind of view, logistics is incalculable and often a book with seven seals.

In the meanwhile, Peter prefer Larissa´s concept and not the traditional way: "make or buy". Buyer and dispatch manager feel outvoted. Unjustly, there is no right to vote. Which view of logistics provides the greatest benefit? Thinks Peter. They are well advised to answer them independently and transparently. But how?

Larissa brings the good old cost-benefit analysis into the game. It helps when there are several options on the table. Instructions can be found on the Internet. At Virtuell.AN, the focus is on awareness raising. After that they can carry out the field of the logistics in the project.

Reconnaissance is tedious and takes time. Depending on the constellation, there are larger and smaller stones in the way. Furthermore, such an undertaking requires money. Normally, it´s doesn't comes out of a project. Their budget depends on the mission anyway, and that's just what's missing. Just al little time is left for "strategy workshops" shortly before the project starts.

Reconnaissance possibly causes pain. At least you get clarity. For example, how logistics works in line with the project and the business plan. It may be painful to get to the bottom of the influence of logistics in a company. For example, what if logistics in the "4.0 format" contributes more to the company's return than the previous orientation. At the latest in that moment, the topic moves to the management. Larissa plans to talk with Peter about it. Her motives on the way to Logistics 4.0 are clear: growth, efficiency, influence, knowledge, costs, security and cooperation.

In a previous project, Larissa had evaluated, the orientation of logistics in the variants 1.0 to 4.0. In the beginning some players there knew just as little about logistics. The basic tenor there: "We have nothing to do with that". In fact, this statement is finding – well formulated in a legally secure manner - in many business conditions. If everyone likes this, the gaps in the logistics systems will become more numerous. Coordination efforts will increase.

Larissa's cost benefit analysis provide food for thought: for example, on the appreciation of logistics in the company. She rated four answers to the question "what does logistics mean for you":

Take your choice:
- "Logistics equals transportation",
- "...is a cost nuisance."
- "...is State of the Art" organized or
- "...is a competitive factor".

She asked another question about the organization of logistics in the plant, project or group. Again, she evaluated four statements:
-   "Logistics is exclusively transport, storage, handling",
-   "„... is a cross-sectional function in the company and serves to coordinate the flow of goods and information",
-   ".... has coordination and design tasks along the supply chain of the company",
- "...networks all logistics chains in the company's value chain".

And again, what is your opinion?

The values show the opportunities, risks and new scopes for action. In any case, such an analysis generates topics that offer an exclusive guide to logistics design.

No wonder, there are others on Larissa's list, which in principle resonate in every company:

- What influence does logistics have on goals, departments and key figures of your company?
- What effect do certain forms of organisation and their orientation have?
- Which logistics goals stand in the way: For example, standardization is hindered by differentiation. Prevention avoids capacity utilization. The first place in costs is only partially profitable, if there is no turnover.
- Uniqueness, agility and reflex are real goals in the project.
- However, when are lead times possibly more important than the ratio of logistics costs to total costs?
- When is "outsourcing" more important than the quality and reliability of data?
- Is transparency just as important as delivery reliability and stocks?

Difficult questions that can be supplemented as desired. But they also provide surprising insights into logistics and its benefits.

How does it work with the following theses that produces such an analysis?

- It is not the warehouse and dispatch departments that show the greatest benefit for logistics.
- Design and purchasing brings more values in use for logistics.
- In-house logistics" contributes more to the return on investment for your company than "outsourcing".
- In their case, flexibility in logistics achieves the higher benefits compared to standardization and cost leadership.
- Innovation and prevention are more beneficial than the desire to standardize.
- New options beyond transport, storage and handling become visible.
- Logistics improves the development of the organization in your company.

Only the respective scope for action is to be determined.

Back in the office, the project plan moves back into Larissa's field of vision. A paragraph abruptly stops her strategic thinking. The day-to-day business catches her up. The contracts for the transport of the 15 robots are on the agenda. The conditions stipulate that transport is to be provided "ex works" to the place of installation. The own parent company acts as the client. So, the project transports for the mother. Who came up with the idea?

The same applies to the products. Larissa knew them from her first interview. Coated steel components: 27 meters long, seven meters high, two meters wide. 50 tons in weight and equipped with many highly sensitive attachments. Their supply chain extends into Eastern Europe. A contract manufacturer in Eastern Germany manufacture the steel frames. The Bavarian branch of the parent company assembles the attachments. The project transports. In this case they are going in to the role as self-employed freight forwarder and a full liability. Not to be seen in the contract is far and wide the usual insurance for the transport or the exclusion of liability.

The deliveries follow the sequences of the construction site. The trucks loads are assembled immediately after arrival: into a construction that serves as a suspension railway for the future factory.

That was the plan. On paper, a very nice production network appears. A correspondingly large number of suppliers and the construction site must be orchestrated. Among them is also the one who provides the suspension railway. If one single part doesn't work out, then is standing either a supplier or the entire construction site. Trouble is for sure.

The plan provides further information: Seven weeks prior to installation, the project company must commission the transport in writing. The drafters of the agreement left it open whether land or sea transport was preferred. Further statements are noted: "For the calendar week which is determined, the project company orders the transports for shipment. They provide also in time a guarantee for the purchase of the transport and lifting equipment in the amount of 700,000 €. The alarm bells start to ring in Larissa's head. She confronts Ethan about the facts of this case. His succinct answer: "Find a forwarding agent". He deliberately ignores the second part and the ball flies back into her field. Larissa now sits again and alone in her worldwide logistics corridor: With the view on the haystack to search the needle it:

There are almost 16,000 freight forwarders in Germany. How do freight forwarder and project become a couple?

Couple dancing allows several options for a balanced whole:

- a fixed choreography with guidance,
- only through guidance
- or through pure improvisation.

The leader is in this sense the logistician of the project. The leader is the freight forwarder. The movement is indicated by precise time pulses. Consequently, technical, methodological and social compatibility is required. Otherwise each other stand on your feet's.

Just like in the theatre, most of the action takes place behind the scenes. The project team in the logistic auditorium is happy when the consignments are over the finish line. In the background many are pulling the strings: Shipping companies, container packing stations, port operation companies, haulage contractors, shipbrokers, customs agents and several authorities such as the port authority, customs or the city office for the approval of heavy transports.

In this light Ethan's message "Find a new carrier" appears in a strange setting.

Ethan apparently works according to the motto: "Logistics works when nobody notices anything". But when the baton falls, the project team is immediately under pressure. Logistics becomes quickly to a pain in the neck. Depending on how the orders with the forwarding agents are then to be arranged. Stand there either empty-handed or with influence.

The most common logistics service providers are freight forwarders, ship owners and warehouse keepers. With their trucks, ships and warehouses, they stand at the visible tip of the iceberg. Important is who acts as a carrier. At first it´s the entrepreneur who undertakes to carry out a transport by means of a transport contract. This may be the purchase contract with the corresponding delivery clauses. The general rules in Germany stipulate that the forwarder arranges the shipment. For the time being, there is no mention of implementation. The key is the question above: Who is the carrier? At the first, the project is it, even if a forwarding agent has been commissioned.

The freight forwarder is authorized to carry out the transport of goods in self-delivery. Only when he makes use of it, does he obtain the rights and obligations of a carrier. In addition to the remuneration for his activity as a forwarding agent, he will demand the usual freight. If he owns trucks to carry out the transport, he is also a transport contractor. Quasi everything from one source with corresponding interests.

The logistics assigns the warehousing the task of bridging time. The storage contract obliges the warehouse keeper to keep the goods. He is trustee of the goods, which requires a special relationship of trust. Larissa was forced to store her furniture because the new apartment was not ready. This is indeed a private business story. But they generate the same sleepless nights as in the project, if parts are missing or damaged at the end.

Other players are on stage, if the path leads over the ocean. The spotlight is now on for the shipowners. The Section 476 of the German Commercial Code (HGB) says to him: He is the owner of a ship which operated by him for the purpose of acquisition by sea. The shipping company is primarily concerned with the equipment, manning, maintenance and operation of its ship(s). In the real estate sector, this would be almost comparable to facility management. The charter party would thus be the distant relative of the tenant contract for an apartment.

If the shipping company deals with the acquisition of cargo, it becomes a charterer. In this context, he is not a carrier, but her acts as a broker or agent under commercial law. The representative of the shipowner on board a ship is the captain. He shall be authorized to carry out all transactions and legal acts, which the operation of the vessel normally entails. His competence also extends to the conclusion of freight contracts and the issuing of bills of lading.

The different roles of the actors, and even the commissioning, is often a controversial point. It´s the same with Ethan and Larissa. They discuss the orders and interfaces. Ethan argues that the responsibilities and all liability issues should be regulated through the transport contracts. Larissa's wishes to keep as many threads in her hand as possible, although this means more work.

Suspicion often resonates in such conversations. Larissa always gets in such kind of situation the feeling that the other person suspects she wants to expand her mission. The project manager naturally thinks about the amount of his expenses for third parties. Moreover, the reasoning always leads over one admission: Others have it better under control! This confession requires courage. If, on the other hand, the bottleneck is just around the corner, the order is born out of necessity. In this case, the invoice of the external party, even in the amount, is usually not questioned.

However, this is not the end of the matter. Above them still hovers the duty of transport. Make or buy, the classic question, must be answered. The choice of transport modes, the routes as well as the following entrepreneurs is gladly left to the purchasing department with the statement "buy". As you know, Larissa would prefer to do that herself. Closing with the one who offers the best price is not always the first choice. Many agree with this truism. But most of the time they do it as usual. Especially the very ones who must not deal with the consequences. Larissa preferred then to fall in with the one she selected herself.

Many freight forwarders also respond to numerous activities with a reflex answer: "We do that too". In this case the field will be cultivated. For the sale of insurance, packaging, storage, customs clearance and so on. They prefer also the coordination overall, but under her roof. As mentioned above, the project team sits then as spectators in the hall. Ethan's head was spinning. The dance moves into a tango, with the carrier in the leadership position.

Without doubt, many tasks require control and co-ordination. The operative implementation handles interfaces between ports, airports, forwarding agencies, warehouses and factories. Ethan seems the delimitation of tasks extremely diverse. Forwarding agents can be found for air and sea freight, customs, rail, ports and airports, with and without trucks and many more. Others see their hobbyhorse in certain regions, groupage, projects, containers or heavy cargo.

Larissa continues: "Many works alone for the transport. The only thing that counts: Reach the best possible utilization of your own vehicles. Just the view, that the ideal transport is the one that is avoided, makes most people shudder. They lead directly to a view of the mountain of credit and leasing agreements. This creates the natural pressure of freight forwarders, haulage contractors and ship-owners; on project managers and others. Her single interests, to carried out as much transports as possible.

"The question of capacity utilization inevitably leads to being standardization of current transport systems. Identical containers, pallets and packaging are interchangeable and transport masses. It is precisely this fuels the war of prices and distribution. However not only the transport modes are standardized. The same applies to the processes in transport, storage and handling. Shift systems and working regulations are just as fixed," says Larissa.

In their opinion, these aspects reduce flexibility and reaction in projects. The most is pressed into the standard, first. Until special solutions and bypasses are built to eliminate the bottlenecks, everything against surcharge of course. Some market participants are suspected to be waiting for it alone.

On the other hand, if customers declare individuality and flexibility to the standard, many organizations in logistics reach their limits. But the system is robust. They try to drive the individual solution into the standards. Logistics managers, like Larissa found themselves in a dilemma again. One millstone forces standard because of the prices. The other pushes for flexibility and redundancy. Of course, this is just one conflict in the frame of the logistical objectives. Just one would be too little. We have more.

Logistics one, two, three... and four: How find project managers and logistics managers a common line?

Ethan and Larissa try the well-known question first: "Who does what"? As usual with software products, they use numbering by versions and assign them. Asset orientation is a further aid.

Logistics 1.0 is if dealers or manufacturers operate a fleet or a warehouse themselves. Companies that rely on logistics 1.0 can be found in many places. Amazon is a prominent example. The solution makes perfect sense if products and quantities match the vehicle fleet and warehouses.

The solution is also an option for your project. According to the contract you are already the carrier. If they hire drivers and trucks, they transport in self-entry. Ethan and Larissa see this as an option, after a long discussion. Ethan says, but just in case of emergency,

They assign the "Logistics 2.0 format" to companies whose business purpose is the utilization of vehicles and real estate. This includes haulage contractors, container truckers, regional freight forwarders and shipping companies. The variant is useful if you buy directly. Anyway, Larissa strives to turn as many set screws as possible by herself. She is aware that the decision of „go" or " no go" not only in this matter was moving towards Peter. It´s a strategic decision of the management level.

In the next step, they associate the term contract logistics with Logistics 3.0. For Ethan is one-stop shopping the best solution. You fix a contract and that's it. All logistic tasks in the project would have been done with it. However, he wouldn't put his hand in the fire. After he had met Larissa. The greater the distance to the markets, the greater the need for organization and control in the transport and supply chain. Reminded Larissa.

The version Logistics 4.0 is new for Ethan at the first moment. So, the discussion drags on until they agree: 4.0 stands for the independent control of logistics over the entire workflow of a company in real time. This means that not technology seal the fate of workflows, it´s the other way around. What consequences does this have for your project? Develop more organization! This gratifying finding is followed by the next question: How to integrate Logistics 4.0? Ethan and Larissa see the picture of the dispatch manager in front of themselves. Personally, he's a great guy. However, would they succeed taking him away from his stable and well-established working boat to a fragile project racing yacht? And one of the latest generations?

The path leads them again and without a doubt to the management. If they succeed in triggering new impulses for the logistics strategy of Virtuell.AN, the project will gain. Accordingly, they prepare a conversation with Peter.

The image of the famous iceberg serves as a guide. At the top are the classic functions of transport, storage and handling. The workflow of a company is found in the depths of the sea. At the top end the wind of the logistics market is blowing: driven by the battle for prices and big business. Below the waterline, people, information and material produce the goods for it. Diversely currents within the company provide the flow. Wind and current move the whole thing, just here the iceberg. Together they produce waves. Their magnitude depends on the interplay or opposition of the forces. If somebody influence the currents in the company so that disturbances occur, the icebergs first collide under water. At first invisible for transport, storage and handling at the top of the same. It´s too late for logistics. The baton falls. More precisely, the consignment that usually sprints from hand to hand. She ends up in the warehouse. When in doubt, the stop for the whole follows. Depending on how high the waves are beating in the project. They hit logistics all the harder and immediately afterwards transport, storage and handling.

Two days later, after the conversation, crackling silence fills the room. Peter is silent. Ethan looks out of the window. He can see the dense rain very well in front of the trees. They protect the office building a little from the street noise. Larissa is thinking about her just finished lecture. What went wrong? The first sheets arrange the basic terms. They prepare the field of common understanding and presents examples from everyday life as well as from projects. Additional they show what the others are doing. They set the course for the logistical inventory.

Finally, Larissa explained the interrelation between the project and the logistics market. She ends with two questions:

What is expected from logistics?

Why is projects fail?

The first serves for classification, the second as a wake-up call. Afterwards occurs the mentioned calm. Ethan looks like he's doing a balancing act. What's tore him in two halfs? He already understood that he had to take care of the logistics. He liked the subject as much as the way to the dentist. In this respect, prophylaxis is probably an accurate comparison against painful experiences.

On the other hand, his project moves within the framework of the logistics practices of Virtuell.AN. It's useless, if he suddenly finds himself on an island with new ideas and methods. Surrounded by the keepers of the existing. All connections to the rescuing mainland are cut off by them, if he targets new shores too quickly. Unless bridges are built from there. The first bridge builder is in his opinion, Peter.

Meanwhile, the past catches up Peter. He ought to have known better. His studies in mechanical engineering and his training as a customs investigator allow him to look ahead. Despite of the many terrible experiences. A customs investigator sees rather the semi-darkness of the industry. They drove him to that group of people who say: "Logistics, I don't care with it." It's naive to think. It's only a matter of time before someone puts their finger in the wound. Larissa as an external has the guts.

Peter is not sure. How to organize their logistics and how to use the potentials? He admits to himself that logistics is not clearly in focus of his management. The real processes are not very transparent and comprehensible. Ethan will also not shoulder the task alone. To be move the logistics in his project on the state of the art.

Peter gives himself a jerk. At least he finds his language again. "Okay," he says. "Only to understand: We have totally different views and images of logistics in our heads, right?" Larissa and Ethan nod. That's right. "All that's missing is a common understanding, right?" They nod again. Peter try it with a threatening tone of voice: "Do you think that our logistics need a renovation or at least should be put to the test bench?". They were not impressed by his tone. Nod, three times consent.

As always, he is not sure: Do the employees act out of their own conviction? Otherwise is the following motto also conceivable: "Reporting makes you free and burdens the supervisor". In this case, he estimates that at least eighty percent of them speak from their own convictions.

"Is logistics part of our core competence?" He thinks aloud.

"Crystal clear YES!", Larissa beats him to it.

Originally, he was aiming for a crystal clear "no". But Peter replies: "We haven´t seen it in that way so far", and adds, "if we have the requirement, then we need more knowledge. Furthermore, the colleagues are to be brought on board. This needs a way in order to do not get shipwrecked or go around in circles after taking off. What do you think?"

"That sounds like the beginning of a plan," Ethan replies.

Larissa is only hoping that they weren't see her restlessness. It's too thin for her. "More knowledge means informing, training, learning," she says. Experience knowledge is doesn't to readable. For this, people are indispensable who are willing to share their wealth of experience.

Ethan thinks on his own behalf: "I think it is best to gather knowledge for our project in the first step. I am interested in example, if methods of project management are compatible with those of logistics management. I hope this is way to avoid misunderstandings, Larissa."

"In any case, the issue of digitization will catch up with us," Peter continues, "I don't see any other way.

We must check which instruments of the so-called digital transformation are usable for us.

"We are most likely an be able to gather experiential knowledge from a retrospective perspective," Larissa muses, "I mean when we look at old projects or business models and ask ourselves how they work with the new. Then it'd be like a back to the future game."

"Okay, we'll tackle that," Peter suddenly decides spontaneously, "I'll play the 'back to the future' game. Ethan will try to harmonize the methods. Larissa investigate the crystal ball of digitization. We will meet again in two weeks on this topic. Then we hopefully able to see what action radius for the logistics is currently possibility for us".

Time-out: Logistics is everyday life! Everyone is happy when they hold the ordered package in his hands. Some people would like to have logistics concepts like recipes on the Internet.

Elisabeth jumped out of bed this morning and chased into the company. Otherwise, she won't staff her reception until 8:30. Today she is a driven one. Urgent businesses must be done. Otherwise, Eastern runs to a disaster. If she does not have the ordered package in her hands.

One of her many part-time jobs in reception are the parcel services. She calls at 14:00, gives up the number of packages and at 16:00 everything is done. Basically, she is surprised that there were always five of them: Five services that bring or pick up small packages with small lorries. But well, today she's out on her own.

Her parcel service has been showing the same status for days. Real panic ensued when she read in the paper yesterday: "Many thousands of packages linger in the external warehouse of the parcel service". The automated sorting plants are as overloaded as the motorway networks at Easter. Her fear is growing. The Carrera racetrack for her son, she won't get there in time. Not only her son would be disappointed. Her husband is also waiting for the gift.

Shortly after seven she ordered the second track. Just to be on the safe side. In another web shop and with express delivery for the next day. A little relieved she asks herself: How does it work? She didn't know where her order was landing and where the goods were coming from.

From a driver of a parcel service she knows that he delivers her parcels to a local forwarding agency. From there drives trucks the collected shipments to a distribution center, 60 kilometers far away. A fully automated system sorts the parcels for other trucks. They transport them to the receiving locations. The first ones leave at 19:00 for example in the direction of Munich. They arrive there around four o'clock in the morning for unloading. From five o'clock on-wards, other drivers load her smaller trucks for their local transport routes. The distribution is clocked by the opening hours of the receivers and the time zones in which the pedestrian zones are to be used.

Elisabeth's employer, Virtuell.AN, is a manufacturing company and not a web shop. But here the same applies: distribution logistics for one is procurement logistics for another. This includes all activities for supplying the production with raw materials, auxiliary materials, operating supplies, semi-finished products and purchased parts. Just like the dispatch of finished products and spare parts.

She did not know why the responsibility for the parcels had ended up at her reception of all places.

The colleagues in the dispatch department would be equally suitable. They receive or send all other deliveries. How turbulent the dispatch department is depending on how many machines the sales department sells.

She can only guess what they pay for the shipments per parcel. The purchasing department will negotiate the tariffs, hopefully. Only once there was a real bang. At that time, she already noticed that the boxes of the consignments were getting bigger and bigger. The room behind her reception was simply bursting at the seams. However, the weight and number remained unchanged. It seemed as if only the boxes had blown up.

By chance came out: A trainee works in the shipping department. He liked the new paper padding machine. Withdrawn in the corner of the warehouse, he filled the cavities of the boxes with fun. Always chose larger ones for the smallest items. Many packages they tested had nine times of the actual item packaging. No wonder that packing material was constantly being bought. More vehicles drove into the yard because the previous ones were simply full. Filled by the carefree packer at the consignors.

Whatever, the web shop is now telling her that the new Carrera racetrack is under construction. The ordering address was in the middle of Berlin. Elisabeth continues her research on "web maps". There was no dispatch warehouse to be seen, in the middle of Berlin. She googles and stumbles over a remarkable paragraph. She reads it out loud twice until she understands:

"The scope of tasks and the conception of procurement logistics are equally relevant for distribution logistics. Depending on the type of division of work in the logistics network, the tasks fall either into the area of procurement or distribution logistics. In this interplay it is essential that the distribution logistics specialists are informed about the customer's procurement logistics.

Elisabeth asks herself. Is an order in a web shop, like her **Carrera racetrack the procurement logistics problem of everyone?** Whereby she puts her case in the hand of the distribution logistics of the web shop. At the click of the mouse, she releases her logistics package for the "outsourcing". Without knowing what's happening. Shopping on site and taking it with you is easier. This means she has her procurement logistics under control. Which solution is more convenient is clear when you hold the package in your hands. Right now, the next toy store is more tempting for her. If only to revive the past anticipation of Easter.

She continues to browse the net: *"The distribution logistics strategy depends on whether production is for the anonymous market ("make to stock") or for selected customers ("make to order").* Elisabeth suspects that the track is in stock. She is anonymous for the web shop and therefore a "make to stock" case.

She continues in scrolling: *"Distribution logistics influences sales success in the consumer goods sector directly. The close relationship forces the harmonization of logistic systems between manufacturer and logistics service provider. Missed sales, for example due to shortages, affect all levels of the sales channel. On the other hand, the reduction of costs is based on the minimization of inventories. The consolidation of storage levels and stockless transshipment points such as cross docking or transshipment points lead to decreasing stocks".*

Oh dear, so complex? She didn't study this and now it´s caught her in the everyday life. **She would like to see logistics concepts like the recipes on the Internet.**

Although this is no guarantee that it will work. Just like cooking. But at least it gives her an idea of what is happening. Elisabeth continues to think about it: "A stockless transfer point at home is often the refrigerator. Several times of a day she runs around the corner for every little part. The supermarket is their central warehouse! Her man and her son want´s only pick up in the refrigerator.

Okay, the number of her paths is increasing. The advantage, there's more money in the bag. Compared to the times when bulk buying was piling up in the basement. Elisabeth is become aware that her paths to the supermarket, basically go through as one of these new "same day" or "same hour delivery" services. After all, her transportation costs nothing.

Elizabeth keeps scrolling. The next paragraph explains why the mega-high shoe boxes have been standing in the landscapes about 15 years. They call themselves high-bay warehouses. Later the new warehouses are not be so high anymore. For that they eat away the ground. Not only along the highways.

The following sentence says: *In this context there are questions regarding the site planning:*

- *How many locations are required?*
- *Where are the optimal ones in the Distribution System?*
- *Over how many distribution levels is the delivery to the customers proceeding?*
- *From which site are which customers are supplied?*

The advantages of a central warehouse are: Europe-wide distribution, lower safety stock per item, higher availability, easier replenishment and warehouse management. The transport and transit times to the customer are higher because the shipments are fed into the regional networks of the freight forwarder.

Elisabeth takes notes for better understanding: If the central warehouse (supermarket) was combined with regional hubs (refrigerator), a 24-hour service (for your men) is possible in most cases without a stock in the refrigerator. Independent of this, there are local distribution centers with and without central warehouses. They enable faster delivery (her son's bedside table).

Local stocks are adjusted to requirements with ever better forecasts. Articles with a low turnover rate (milk) are stored centrally. Articles with a high turnover rate (chocolate) are deposited locally. In addition, the network will grow more easily with the customer base, it said. She knows it from home: Before her son's friends spend the night with him, her junior automatically stashes a lot of chips. Locally deposited in the bedside table.

Once again it becomes clearness why many warehouses spring up out of the ground in recent years. Elisabeth provides the reasons herself. Her own behavior as a consumer is responsible. She read in a newspaper: **Like residential and office properties, logistics real estate is now considered a separate asset class. Without them, no shipment will reach the finish line.**

But there is also the talk of minimum wages, citizen protests and land consumption. The dilemma is obvious: everyone wants fresh goods from the supermarket and weekly market day after day. On the other hand, nobody is asking for delivery traffic and certainly not by truck from 05:00 in the morning.

"Good morning, Elizabeth". She is shocked for moment. "Good morning, Peter." Her boss is standing in front of her reception desk. She usually sees him when she parks. Every morning he tries to hit the parking box with his 250 HP sedan. He is very creative in this matter and works without a learning curve. Today he took her by surprise. The moment of shock is followed by a moment of time pressure. She's late. The meeting room must be prepared. Coffee, tea, biscuits for four people. At home they use "Skype" for such kind of meetings. Her three sisters would otherwise only see her at Christmas. Just the travelling and all the preparation. In addition, sometimes you have something to say to each other and sometimes you just don't. She admires the same game in the conference room. Out of politeness alone, many conversations are dragged over the 45-minute limit. When she brings the second pot of coffee halfway through, this fact is often already clearly visible.

In front of the coffeemaker it reverberates what she has just read. *Another factor that leads to changes in logistics or distribution networks is the life circle of the products. It´s* buzzing in her head. Many of them are shooting stars and fads. *When these are over, the logistics networks will be redesigned, and sites will be reassessed.* Was to read.

She never understood these systems. The suspicion germinates stronger as she set the table. **She did it yourself.** It is not only the Carrera racetrack, which has been ordered twice. It requires additional truck tours for the returned parts. So far, this has not been any importance to her. The right of return is included in the price. Her remorse gets another stitch. The large Internet retailers are operating separate logistics networks for their return alone. It is worrying that it is often cheaper to scrap the returned goods. While the alternative is more expensive: Check, pack and re-introduce into the distribution logistics just for the resale. What happens to her racetrack if she sends it back?

Okay, that's enough. She must go. She forces the apprentice into the reception. Shortly after half past nine Elisabeth buys the third racetrack. The one which is already waiting in the toy store. At 10:00, she cancels the second one. The first one will be donated when it´s arrives. This is their spontaneous act to relieve the logistics networks before Easter.

"Good morning, Elizabeth," Ethan calls out in a good mood through the spring sun. She hurries past him in the parking lot. Okay, her "Morniiiing" seems a little rushed. Ethan turns back towards the office. Yesterday evening he had succeeded in giving the first concrete form to his task:

Act Two

Design project and logistics management compatible

It is always impressive. In project management there seem to be methods like sand on the beach. Their properties generate terms such as agile, Six Sigma", Scrum or Critical Chain. Ethan is surprised that the same applies to logistics. It says, eight R`s, just in time, just in sequence, pull and push, hub and spoke and much more. How does it fit all together? Which serve their purpose?

The first on his list is the principle of baton. Larissa and Ethan talk about how the baton, here the consignments, sprints from hand to hand. If it falls, it symbolically stores. The project chain is interrupt.

Ethan knows principle of baton from athletic training. While he is waiting for the baton handover, the smooth handover will be prepared. He looks back to realize when the delivery will be expected. He starts running in time so that the good is handed over at the right speed. Once the baton or shipment has been taken over, the only task is to hand it over to the next runner as soon as possible or to bring it to the finish. Nobody tolerates it. Even not the spectators, if the runner takes a break in between or does other tasks, such as participating in the long jump competition.

Shipment tracking systems serve the baton principle. Everyone can view where the baton is, that they have ordered, by mobile phone, laptop or tablet. This is not possible without gaps and in real time. Only the connection points are recorded, i.e. the factory gate, the loading and unloading or the front door. The interfaces are of little help when tracking large components in European or worldwide transport. Especially if components are on the way with a length of 20, 30 meters or more. In such case additional information about their position in space is important. You often get the receipt, if it's too late. Ethan remember many invoices that quantify the immense expenses of the service providers. For example, relocation with cranes and heavy transporters is expensive if way to the components are misplaced by others. The same applies to the lush lanes. The so-called tractory curves show already in the planning phase which space the vehicles need for their maneuvers. They are usually kept free. If the delivery cycle stumbles due to blocked parts or paths, the construction site is quickly brought to a standstill.

Otherwise, disputes or delayed payments trigger similar processes.

The focus is therefore on the correct communication with the predecessor. The handing over of the task and the timely preparation determine the start. This is done before the precursor does its job. Thus, the overall speed must be maintained. The order will be processed as quickly as possible. If you finish faster, you activate the successor.

Like the coach in athletics, the project and logistics management must dose the tasks. Four times 100 meters is not four times 400 meters in a relay sprint. If you are carried off the track in the curves it costs distance and the correction of the handover at the point. If you stumble when changing there is a risk of damage. For people and goods.

Ethan works constantly in relay races, the project company also. Among other things are there the steel sections for the foundation. These are to be collected from the supplier ex works. The conclusion of the transport contracts is already scheduled. Only the essential data´s are missing. It seems pitfalls and security arrangements are built into the project plan. Depending on the point of view. It is salient that they only read something about the start and end points of the transports. Neither the route nor the mode of transport is fixed when the prices are negotiated.

A later comparison of the solution with the target is obsolete from the beginning. Thinking the process from the end, no way. The question of the best transport solution is still open. Comparisons with distance, missing. The data provides parts lists, articles, components and assemblies. Without them there is a calculation of prizes in transport impossible.

The project plan suggests by contrast security. It states that the acceptance of the access road and the parking areas for the cranes is scheduled six to eight weeks before the construction starts. Accordingly, vehicles and cranes must be determined earlier especially for heavy transport. The project explained Larissa is responsible for unloading. For the transports are the most suppliers responsible. The latter is read between the lines of the project plan.

Moreover, it appears that the designers of the contract had the just-in-time concept in mind. Means, the shipment is made available to recipients exactly when it`s needed. For projects with their uniqueness is this an idealistic, if not a dangerous idea thinks Ethan.

He notes another insight: The baton almost always marches on the critical path in projects. This delicate path is followed by the caravan of tasks that are directly interdependent. Naturally, everyone strives to dress warmly in a project. You protect yourself with time buffers and create legroom. Buffers and legroom's become a part of the project time. Everyone builds their own time buffer. For this Ethan puts his hand into the fire. Accordingly, these accumulate over the number of tasks and people.

If one annexes the buffers and puts them at the end of the project, there is a chance to shorten the whole project. Furthermore, other paths can be identified as genuinely critical. In Ethan's understanding, this means translated for logistics: Each buffer is a stock. The lower the number, the less time is bridged.

Despite everything, as in the relay race, the logistician will probably always find himself on the critical path. If somebody don´t play with open cards, bottlenecks or disturbances bring the baton into the stock. If is the cow off the ice, the pressure immediately rises to the boiling point again: lost time must be caught up quickly by bridging of the rooms. Logistics meets all tasks of bridging space and time. In the project plan, as mentioned above, the most information is to be found between the lines, but for this in all passages.

The classic project management determined the scope first. Times, costs and resources depend on it. In contrast of this agile methods define cost and time budgets at the beginning. After that they think about how and which requirement is implemented. They accept generally that one-time or first-time events are not foreseeable. Many projects are too complex to forecast their progress in a comprehensive plan or contract. At the beginning of the project, a significant part of the requirements and solutions will rather appear as white spots on the map. For this it´s important to equip employees with methods and to deal with this. Scrum is such a working method.

Scrum is originally found in American football and English rugby. The teams work on the pitch as self-organized units. From the outside they are only given the generally directions. On site, they decide for themselves how to reach their destination. So, how the consignment or the ball the line hits. The opponent disturbs with external events. New situations must be solved quickly.

Ethan wonders if and in what way will this method boost logistics. So far it was not his intention to test this approach in the project. Scrum focuses on the pillars of transparency, review and adaptation. In Ethan's view transparency in logistics means transparency of the market, structures and processes. It is certainly necessary that observers share a common understanding. This is precisely where he sees a contradiction or even an obstacle: many business models live in the logistics market from the inscrutability of the market. In this respect, Ethan believes that the adversities by using scrum in the logistics of projects outweigh.

Another pivotal point in Scrum is the sprint. This means that a finished, usable and deliverable product is produced within a period of two to four weeks. In Ethan's opinion, such a product is, for example, the logistics concept for his project. Designing a logistics plan in the sprint of the Scrum method. That's a starting point.

Further cornerstones are not only relevant in scrum: Courage, focus, openness and respect. All who are involved become more competent about these values. They personally commit themselves to achieving these goals. In this case, the team works in a self-organized, interdisciplinary manner and decides for itself how to do its work.

These interdisciplinary teams have all skills needed to finish the job. They are independent of persons outside the team. To develop a logistics concept expert from the fields of logistics, law, IT, construction and purchasing are involved. The number of members is four, with a maximum of nine.

So much for the theory: Ethan wonders if they are already ready at Virtuell.AN to design a concept for logistics with the help of the Scrum method. He comes up with harmful multitasking. The term multitasking has a positive connotation according to general opinion. It refers for the ability to perform several tasks simultaneously. The other side of the coin begs the question: what dosage is needed to make multitasking harmful? Harmful multitasking is a common term in project management. It´s guilty when a work is interrupted in favors of another task. The motives are human: to please everybody is a very clear reason. Furthermore, project managers usually compete for the scarce resources in the company. Line departments serve in central functions as service departments. Matrix organizations provide employees for projects. Usually without letting the threads out of her hands.

Even Ethan uses the best-known method: the one who shouts loudest is the first to be served. The employees of the departments then jump from one situation to the other. It is clear to everyone that the set-up times cost time and money.

Ethan is looking for an abstract example to illustrate it for his people. The day-to-day business comes not into the consideration. Pointing out measures and errors is not the current matter.

For his model case he outlines three projects. One each in Mallorca, Menorca and Ibiza. It is planned to develop the logistics for the project on Mallorca in the first five weeks. Afterwards to be active in Ibiza and subsequently in Menorca. Ibiza and Mallorca are already under time pressure. Menorca is relaxed. Relevant data and requirements are missing in Palma. The development is interrupted. The project managers in Menorca and Ibiza are pushing to meet their schedules. One for a good reason, the other just to proforma. This shows why situation-Islands are created in multi-project management, says Ethan to himself.

In his example, the logisticians interrupt their work on Mallorca and travel to Ibiza. The customer demands result in order to adjust the screws in his own logistics system. The interruption should only be short. However, the data for Mallorca are still missing. The logisticians travel on to Menorca and start their work there.

At the end of the third month, everything is finished in Menorca. Contrary to the plan. In Ibiza complains the project manager about the drastic difference between net-working-time and throughput time. The latter is now three and a half months instead of the planned five weeks. He declares that he will just pay for the hours, which were done in five weeks. He cuts the bills angrily and rather arbitrarily. Over this way, he provokes additional work in the administration area and new negotiation dates on the conditions.

In addition, the set-up times and travel costs are increase from and to the situation Iceland's. The logistics concept for Mallorca will not be completed in the first five weeks. It´s finished after fourth month. Ibiza started earlier but marched across the finish line more than a month later. Menorca, already at the beginning in the green zone. Will be finished about two weeks earlier than calculated. Ethan paints pictures for a presentation. The effects of harmful multitasking become obvious.

The next day Ethan is proud to himself with his another wealth of insight. He notes a further thesis:

Kanban have his home in logistics as well as in project management!

On closer inspection he even knows the method from DIY stores and furniture stores. Here, you don`t take larger items directly from the shelf, just only a card. The product itself is delivered from the warehouse or picked up from there. The remaining number of cards shows the stock level. If the stock has reached the minimum stock level is reordering carried out. This concept is based on the pull principle.

For his project it means: The construction site will be supplied when he himself initiates the order to collect the goods. The rule is the opposite. Suppliers deliver their consignment independently in accordance with his contracts. They follow the push principle. It´s require a progress on the construction site in the moment of the delivery to install the consignment immediately (just-in-time). Otherwise, the receipt area sinks into building material and becomes a warehouse. As already indicated, just-in-time is a functioning concept for well-established processes and mass lot sizes. In the project with its stop and go situations, the term suggests rather exaggerated expectations.

Ethan's thoughts circle back to the Kanban" application in project and logistics. What is if goods are not on the shelves like in a DIY store, but are visible in the network? They have already seen in the SCOR model how simple the visualization is. The management has the basis for steering orders into via Kanban. A pool of tasks will be necessary, clearly. It works like the shelf in a hardware store. The employees get their tasks from the pool. Their general objective is to keep the work flow or in his case the logistics processes. The SCOR model helps to achieve this.

When shopping in a DIY store, cards on the shelf show the stock of goods. If one is taken the purchase process is managed by each person on their own responsibility. It is completed when the goods are paid. Repeat orders or new tasks are initiated by the project management. Ethan sees Kanban as the common denominator for project and logistics. In the best case, he finds a tool to automate the information. That would be a topic of digitization, which Larissa is struggling with.

This task is facing every project manager and logistics manager today. The question to be answered is:

...how operational are the digital instruments?

And how do you approach the subject?

Like starting a new job, Larissa is buzzing with abstract terms. Terms are on the table like digital transformation, platform economy, software as a service, new work and many others. She hopes that digitization will provide one thing above all: the chance to automate information logistics.

Her researches bring a regulatory cycle to the light. It shows a procedure for the determination of requirements and use cases. The actors who designed the cycle were faced with the question of what the seaport of the future would look like. An interesting topic, Larissa thinks. Especially in times of digitalization, artificial intelligence and blockchain.

The regulatory cycle seems to be generally applicable. First, it focuses on the needs, roles and tasks of people. Followed by an examination of the processes and the entire logistics network. In the second step, three further fields are added: they called it critical incidents, greenfield and what if. The fields can be combined in any way and alternately. The mirror is held up to the digitalization. Limits and feasibility must be identified at an early stage.

The critical incidents are considered in terms of positive and negative events. In contrast allows the green meadow an open field of vision. The what if question is rather the most common form. Everyone uses it for critical reviews of innovations and their validity.

It quickly becomes clear that this approach generates a wealth of ideas and possibilities. They are collected without reservation. For the evaluation helps the described cost benefit analysis again. It allows to determine favorites and priorities. At the end the prioritized ideas will be incorporated into a tabular business plan. It provides further findings on economic efficiency and feasibility.

How does the method help the daily business asks Larissa herself? Everyone knows the costs. Who has ever chartered a ship, mobilized a heavy mobile crane or got personnel and equipment up and running. The same applies in the event of an incident. They end up in the e-mail inbox as liability, waiting time calculation and claim immediately. The process is an emergency, because one interface has burst in the network for the moment. The traffic lights light up red for the entire project.

How quickly and with which digital instruments is such a process reanimated? An open question. In principle, it is essential that digital solutions are readily available in a plug and play format. Larissa gets the feeling that this is green field thinking again.

Larissa continues her research. How to describe requirements and processes for digitization? If you know the processes, it´s more than the half rent. On the other hand, present sellers and the internet, the new technologies in general, but for this with impressive prospects for the individual. How fits one into the other? The above-mentioned project to the seaport of the future found the following solution: *Our architectural model shows the static of digital thoughts on the levels of process, networking and technology. Just one bears the burden on proof; the process level.* At this level the power must be put on the road. At the technology level are smart phones, sensors, webcams, apps or data mining software in the shopping basket. Web services, clouds and their adapters provide the network. Larissa formulates her requirements accordingly: The technology can be used flexibly. If they change ships, cranes, components or persons. The target is the monitoring of

several processes from a central location simultaneously. The network level ensures the alignment and
the provision of further information from sensors or
weather data.

Some days later Larissa knows more about the
technical hurdles. The bandwidth and performance
of Internet connections is one point. The minimum
requirement is LTE, later 5G. WLAN has problems
with certain weather conditions. The choice of mobile cameras is equally important. The image forwarding to the encoder and the subsequent upload.
HDMI cables only work reliably for 10 to 15 meters
and offer a trip hazard. SDI cables and technology
seem expensive. WLAN cameras are often config-
ured in such a way that they only set up their own
WLAN network or offers live streaming not at all. So,
topic is the networking of data on the web level with
video streams and sensor data.

What generates the costs? The programming of
the interfaces and codes for networking of the devices. Developing of the dashboards for real-time
analysis. The fees for the transfer of data per use.
The mobile cameras, encoder boxes, IoT sensors.
The media streaming, which is decoded in the upload (per gigabyte and usage) The cloud storage for
the database (per "gigabyte"/per period) as well as

the provision of the database. She never had much to do with IT. Now she is as logistician on the way as broker for digital technologies.

Open questions remain: How many gigabytes are created in total? How much does the corresponding LTE connection cost? Which services are used by the networking platform and what are the costs with the gigabyte turnover in the project? How much does the on-demand video delivery? What does the configuration per action require? How long does it take to program the pre-selected technology? With a status ready for use in the project? Larissa underlines ready for use.

If cloud streaming is too expensive, what are the alternatives? How can costs and benefits be assessed? Live streams of festivals and sporting events are provided. But they require enormous sums of money and are costly. The business management perspective moves into the foreground. If it turns out that the Internet coverage has too many white spots and/or the technology is too expensive, then feasibility is over.

With this insight and a slight sense of giddiness, Larissa addresses the next question: Is the planning phase of projects and especially the risk assessment of processes to be supported by digital instruments? She's hoping to find some sort of toolbox for the operation again.

The so-called toolbox meetings with staff for safety instructions will be given virtually and visually, then. Ideally, they should be evaluated automatically afterwards. The efforts for creating and maintaining method statements as well as the proof of faults and damages will automated. On-site monitoring will be simplified or even centralized. Again, and again are the question arise is it a realistic ideal or a green meadow? Larissa isn't sure. It's clear: In a project it is better if it works. No one will afford experiments.

Before their use a very good statement of reasons must be preceded. If economic reasons are barely tangible becomes it difficult. For Larissa it is conceivable that digital tools could be justified in projects on risk assessment. Larissa finds in the Cloud ones from an old project.

The template of the risk assessment divides a matrix into four categories. It distinguishes between extremely high, considerable, moderate and low risk. Extremely high risks are referred to as catastrophes. Considerable amounts cause considerable damage to personnel or goods. Significant financial losses are in any case to be expected in these stages. Considerable and extremely high risks are excluded and should be avoided as a matter of principle. In this assessment, lower risks generate damage of up to 10,000 euros, while the average effect is up to 100,000 euros.

In the next step is estimated the probability of occurrence per event. Five levels are staggered in: Sure, expectable, possible, rather questionable and unlikely. In the present review is seen in four of the five levels the probability of occurrence of minor hazards. This means it is given a probability of damage. The question remains how often will these occur, for example when 20 ships are loaded?

Larissa moves on to another case. The example evaluates the unloading of 61 ships. They were loaded with mega-large pipes. A graph shows extreme values between six and twelve hours for nine discharges. While it took an average of four and a half hours to handle the other pipes. The additional expenditure was estimated between 3,600 and 18,000 euros per pipe, compared to the average.

From a risk assessment perspective, the probability of occurrence was 14 percent. The interference corresponded to the low and medium range. After all, these were values to be argued: The probability of throwing a six at the dice game is slightly higher at 16 percent. The result destroys the wishes and thoughts of error-free processes again. However, this does not justify digitization in projects.

She continues surfing the cloud and switches files again. A list of participants appears. Apparently, a debriefing session was held with 36 people. It served the exchange of experiences. They talked about learning curves. Spontaneously Larissa starts to calculate. She calculates the time for the appointment as well as for arrival and departure per person with two hours. This results in a total of nine man-days. She puts the man-hour at 50 euros and adds up 3,600 euros for the event. Further protocols shown how many people participated on instructions for occupational safety. It was ten people per loading. She calculates one hour per participant including setup times. For 20 shipments, the total amount is 10,000 euros. One thing leads to another.

She comes across invoices in the next file. The loading was planned by an external service provider. The amount is almost 100,000 euros! The planning runs over four months. They were used to investigate feasibility. For this purpose, were examined the carrying capacity of the quay, water depths in the harbor and other nautical conditions. These are precisely the prerequisites that are necessary for the purchase of ships and cranes. Various checklists, safety instructions and process descriptions were also designed. The documents also include technical proof and expert opinions as well as the already known risk assessment.

They have similar conditions in their project. They have her eyes on a transshipment point by the water. It is also located in a former industrial complex an in the direct vicinity of the construction site. The checklists and descriptions as well as the empirical values delivers many keywords. They offer welcome shortcuts for their own considerations. It´s saves time, because they don't start from scratch. On the other hand, the experience knowledge is only partially usable for her project. They are not spared the creation of specific process descriptions. Afterwards you must do your own risk assessment. Nevertheless, Larissa estimates the gain in knowledge of the evaluation at 20-25.000 Euro. For its own planning, she calculates 80,000 euros now. If the transfer point at the idyllic place on the coast came into question.

Back to digitization. Overall, there are more questions than answers: What limits will digitization place on the project and resources? What opportunities are created? Cost factors are important for the assessment of the operational capability. Costs for equipment, programming and clouds must be calculated exactly. In the end, the decisive factor for Larissa is: How is designed a functioning network between the process and technology levels. Only then does it seem promising to sell digital solutions.

Larissa sums up. The project manager who is faced with his project has no time to decide whether digital instruments can be used or not.

Furthermore, the consideration of the past and the future are speculative and served not a comparative scale. Disruptions or deviations are based in the forecast only on assumptions. The benefit of planned countermeasures remains just as uncertain until they occur. In case of a smooth process, planned emergency measures are obsolete.

The key factor of a retrospective analysis is: Previous experience must process in relation to current applications. It is true the topic lessons learned is outdated for Larissa. In her opinion the term suggests only that you have learned something. Most of the time, the learning of a project procedure is stopped because the staff moves on. The 3,600 Euro example for the review meeting is one such.

Larissa does not consider herself that she be able to put a digital toolbox together. Nevertheless, her competence at the process level is important. She continues with the résumé. Many measures suffer from the paradigm: Everything that must be digitized is digitized. The what-if section in the regulatory circle is on the same page. In her case with the question: What is if you make loading and operational islands visible? The green field idea is transmitted the processing in a central room via video streaming. It seems tempting. Sensors show the exact position in space. Measured values from the cranes and the surrounding weather stations correlate. Procedural descriptions and contracts are available by keyword search. Experts from several disciplines monitor and manage joint measures. The preservation of evidence is automatic. A ray of hope.

In addition, as already mentioned, shipments of this kind are relatively slow. There is just not the task to load 30 containers per hour onto a ship by container gantry cranes. It is unlikely that several faults will occur simultaneously. In today's practice, the surveillance personnel stand at various locations their legs in the well-earned belly. Just to ensure smooth operations.

The personnel and travel costs can only be justified to a limited extent by the feeling of security. The positive outcome, i.e. the smooth processing, as well as the disruption belong to the categories of critical incidents in the sense of the regulatory loop.

It's one back and forth. One for and against. Just as for logistics, Larissa sees not another way to define the strategy for digitization in advance. This gives Peter two construction sites: Determine the strategy for logistics and digitization.

Peter fondly remembers the beginning of his professional career. It allows nostalgic thoughts. That's why he has grabbed the task:

"Back to the Future": From the retro perspective to the rendezvous; gathering experience knowledge for digital and AI systems Three practical examples

The retro perspective is a part of development. He is now in his mid-50s. In ten years, he'll be sailing the seas as a pensioner. Sure, his younger colleagues will learn from their own mistakes. However why should them do it twice? It´s better to avoid them. It is his task to create solutions to remain experiences sustainably usable.

He looks for examples and remembers two world-famous business models. His first: The Round-the-World services in container shipping.

They have nothing to do with their current projects and therefore it is well suited as thinking patterns. It is an advantage that older actors have an even better overview of the cases. They gain with their experience and knowledge. At the same time, Peter is counting on the younger generation to research the facts digitally. Moreover, he is sure that they have ready the digital toolbox more likely. On this basis, a historical example is projected onto the future in a dialogue. Peter's idea behind is that they conduct the conversations without coercion or threat to their daily work. With these thoughts he describes his examples.

The business idea of the Round-the-World services envisaged that eight to twelve container ships of a service would continuously circumnavigate the world. They were of medium size and travelled at the same speed in both western and eastern directions.

The history of the Round-the-World services came to an end after only 15 years, around 1999. A decisive factor was the different market shares and the capacity utilization of the ships on the partial routes.

While capacities were not enough on the race tracks between Europe and America or Europe and Asia, they were partly empty in the Pacific, for example. Competitors, on the other hand, commuted between A and B. They better adapted their capacities to their market shares and routes, with vessels of different sizes. Sometime with ships that were wider than the locks of the Panama Canal. This, today one would say disruptive idea, meant the final off.

What are the chances of survival today? With the knowledge and instruments that digitization provides us. In any case, cargo flows, arrival and travel times are easier to forecast. Logistics networks are also knitted closer. At that time, shipping companies were dependent on their agencies, which were active worldwide. Every single container was acquired analogously by people. Global web-based and always accessible portals for booking did not exist. E-Commerce, Amazon and Co. were hardly imaginable shippers.

While the shuttle services began to put their Post-Panamax ships into service. The Round the World ships remained tied to the lock width of the Panama Canal, which was about 33 meters wide. The economy of scale factor of large ships, which determines the transport costs per box, could no longer be beaten. So far to the history. After his extension, the locks of the Panama Canal will be 49 meters wide and create growth. Furthermore, maritime transport has grown at more than twice of the rate that time. Free trade zones, globalization, the opening of China are the drivers. Peter wonders whether autonomous ships are not predestined for Round-the-World services of the newest kind.

Peter's second example results from a spontaneous question: "Do you know the stories of the cargo ships "Munich" and "Bilderdyk"?" Larissa and Ethan google immediately. The M/V "München" of the Hapag-Lloyd shipping line became world-famous through with its tragic sinking in December 1978. Peter remembers the days before Christmas. The whole nation was grieving. The M/V "München" was for the 62nd time on the North Atlantic route. It shuttled between Rotterdam, Bremerhaven and the American ports of Baltimore, Savannah and New Orleans. In the night when the radio contact broke off, the radio operator reported very bad weather and damage to the ship. Since then, the "München" with its 28-man crew has been missing.

Peter remembers this transport system with awe. During his time as a customs candidate they visited the sister ship, the M/V "Bilderdyk". On the split rear they were shaken like in a moving tram. The enormous gantry crane lifted floating lighters with the size of single-family bungalows on deck. Afterwards, the crane droves over the ship and stowed the mega boxes. The spectator's legs were shaking. During the sinking of the M/S "München", it was assumed that this gantry crane was set into motion in the heavy storm and caused the catastrophe.

The business of transporting floating lighters on ships is called "LASH", Lighter Aboard Ship. They transported goods in large quantities across rivers such as the Rhine and Mississippi and far to the inland. The barges had a length of about 19 meters and a width of 10 meters. Their carrying capacity was just under 400 tones. Instead of the crane on board they were able to do without ports. The classic quays and cranes on land were not used. Loading and unloading was done at anchor in the roadstead. After the barges formed into pushed units. They reached their destinations via rivers and canals. The M/S "Bilderdyk" was in service until end of 2007 and was beached and scrapped on a Chittagong beach in early 2008.

Once again arises the question. What chance would have the business idea today? With new materials and processes, they would be lighter, easier to manufacture. If it is built smaller and equipped with sensor technology, it could be equipped as a floating warehouse with goods assortments. Like warehouses which operate as satellites on the waterways. Today, the needs of people can be better predicted. The integration into the supply and disposal of the population is conceivable. Of course, just in cities and in rural areas with water connections.

The examples undoubtedly provide a contrast to the intentions of Virtuell.AN. However, they lead to the same core question: How could the previous steps be achieved with digital assistance and artificial intelligence?

For the next step Peter is looking for examples that come closer to her project. In their cloud he finds a suitable one. 190 megawatt-sized pipes were delivered by ship. The pipes had a length up to 30 and a diameter of 6 meters. They weighed up to 150 tons.

This is rather a common measure for components in heavy plant construction. The process provides him the desired keywords and comparisons for their project. The pipes only serve as a substitute.

The 61 discharges went smoothly. However, the project was for him in a bad memory. His predecessor stumbled over the story. If he noticed that Larissa was researching in the same file, he was not surprised.

In this case, the supplier procured the ship and delivered to free quay. Discharge was their job. Accordingly, the purchasing department procured stevedoring, cranes, vehicles and personnel. The services were purchased as a package. Prices were negotiated on an hourly basis. The result was 2,400 euros per hour. They were paid according to expenses. It was a key Factor to ensure the supply of the production in the project. They had rented a hall especially for this purpose only 50 meters from the ship's berth.

The order value was two million euros just for the unloading. The evaluation shows that the times for the individual discharges fluctuated considerably. The stevedore invoiced for waiting times 200,000 euros. Around 30 per cent was routes time. The rest was spent for the actual time of unloading. In the end, the report referred to an avoidable potential of 640,000 euros. Provided that the operation is optimally planned and an "all-man maneuver" is possible.

In the end, the analysis costs 40,000 euros. This shows the invoices for planning and monitoring of an external logistics company. Peter honestly admitted to himself: If the offer had landed on his table before the unloading started. He would have found it too expensive. With the reference to the budget and the unknown benefits, a no-go answer is easy in such a situation. Now the information was worth its gold.

The reports states that the vessels were notified five days before arrival. He knew from his time at customs. Loading and unloading is geared to the specific and technical characteristics of the ship. Cargo ships of this type are rarely the same.

The exact arrival was known 24 hours in advance There was enough time for the final planning. This process initially ran smoothly. The quality assurance was often already on board. While the vessel was moving into the optimum position at the quay. After that, the control would also be difficult. The transfer of costs and risks changes from seller to buyer in principle when the pipes are lifted in the ship. After that there was no turning back if obvious defects were not noted beforehand.

Peter continues reading. The wind was gusty. For safety reasons, an additional lifting beam was suspended in the crane. As a result, the crane's ballast was modified to counteract the changed center of gravity. The procedure lasted an hour. It cost 2,400 euros. Before the first pipe was lifted out of the ship, the handling was stopped once again. The pipe waited and hanging in the crane over the pier. The report noted that a self-propelling module transporter (spmt) was missing. He was on its way to the transfer point by truck. A second one was in the production hall but was apparently indispensable.

Meanwhile a discussion broke out on the quay. The surveyor noted. The bearing shells for the pipes were allegedly unusable. Replacements have been procured. Two hours later, the first pipe was lying on the underfloor vehicle delivered up to that point. The vehicle drove a few meters to make room for the next pipe. There were found that the first four of the eight axles went off track. The cargo and the vehicle had a weight of 200 tons in that moment. Further damage was imminent. It was just the worm in it.

Now it was decided, probably from a higher level. The next pipe should be driven with the other underfloor vehicle. Happiness in misfortune meant that the production gave it. The dispatch started up again. While they were transporting the pipes to the storage area. Remaining dunnage and the supports for the pipes were unloaded from the ship. For another 2,400 euros. A little later it was ready. They parked the damaged vehicle in a safe position to unload it on the following day. Peter is wondering if something like this is even plannable. How can the crew be prepared for the unexpected when the worm is inside? But what is, if the worm is brought in from outside for some reason?

At least disruptions are a popular source of money: While the effort for planning was still 25 percent less than estimated, the set-up times were exceeded by two thirds. One reason was the strong wind. The discussion on the quay while the pipe was hanging in the crane cost ten person-hours. The times for unloading the pipes into the stock and manufacturing hall were exceeded by more than 50 percent.

The interruption for the "vehicle search" and the discussion about the bearing shells cost 6,000 euros. The cause for the shells was found in the construction, a calculation error. In total, there was a difference of 21 man-hours. Converts almost three working day. If the employee completes his eight-hour working week. All that for one process. It shows how fast the project budget goes down the brook.

What is to be learned from this? How to deal with this knowledge? With simultaneous knowledge of the digital instruments. Does planning succeed better with a visualizable instrument? Would it be an improvement if quay sides were filmed in advance or scanned to scale? The same applies to ships. As well as for the paths in the surroundings. Evaluate loading and unloading via video streaming and present it to the staff before their start working. Is that a possibility.

Everyone knows from football the video analysis. It serves not only as instructions for work and as an instrument in training, but above all as a guide for safe working. In the event of disruptions, a supervisor intervenes in a decentralized manner to control the situation. Expensive discussions are thus prevented. However, what are the costs and benefits? Is there enough time to install digital tools? Are the numbers of disruptions known to estimate the probability of occurrence?

Time and again, one factor thwarts Peter's thoughts: If processes succeed smoothly, no digital help is needed. The higher the number of expected disturbances, the greater their benefit. From this are to be deducted the cases which cannot be avoided by digital instruments. A complicated formula.

Peter turns to another report. Once again had Larissa beaten him to it. Again, it's about pipes. These have a diameter of three meters. They are between 45 and 60 meters long and weigh up to 150 tons. He clicks on the folder "Offers Cranes": The quotations ranged from 360,000 to 423,000 euros. For a rent over 22 weeks. The prices include mobilization and demobilization, excavator mats and lifting beams. Two shackles with a load capacity of 200 tons were not, nor were the steel cables for attaching the lifting beams. The latter was handwritten on the offers. Fortunately, the reader had noted the exclusions visibly for everyone.

The staff had apparently dealt thoroughly with the planning. Technical and static calculations of the handling and storage area for the crane were available. It had a load capacity of 600 tons in a working area of six meters. Sketches show how it works in the swivel range between the pick-up point of the transporter and the loading point on the ship. This results in the load case, together with the weight of the pipes, the leverage of the delivery and the counterweight. Along the tipping edge of the crane, they determined values between 321 and 356 tones, which impacted on the ground. His bearing capacity was determined by a special soil expertise. A construction of distribution plates with bending-resistant excavator mats and extra poured concrete foundations served to transfer the loads into the ground.

What an effort to handle 120 pipes of this kind. How many thinks to such necessities in the sales phase? In the contract were 20 shipment over sea calculated. With round trip times of 30 to 36 hours between the place of dispatch and destination. The ship was paid by the recipient, i.e. the customer. So, he had nothing to do with the feasibilities and the operations on to the quay side.

Other figures show that the operations lasted on average just under six hours. The stevedore calculated a minimum of eight. The reasoning, again handwritten: The usual port practices regulate the working hours in this way. The costs of planning and control amounted to 1,000 euros per trip. The loading cost an average of 11,000 euros. Peter estimates the charter costs of the ship at 8,000 Euro per day. He puts port costs, such as berthing fees, port dues and pilot at 4,000 euros for the average berthing time. He finds an Image in the documents. It´s presents the operation and the ship very attractively. It cost about 18,000 euros, if he summarizes his notes. In total 360,000 euros for an entire picture gallery with 20 photos of 20 shipments. Essential is, are there any clues as to that digital instruments improve the process? At first sight they are not visible!

Interim balance: The path to digital transformation leads via the lowest common denominator of what is feasible.

Two weeks after their last meeting. Peter is still preoccupied with the news from the previous evening. A court had decided. The working hours of all employees must be recorded now. It worked on the shop floor. How was it like in the office or in the home office? Working time based on trust means two things: trust and working time. Capture means more control. And the trade unionists rejoiced in their interviews: The exploitation of colleagues is now contained. On the other hand, they argued against control and transparency. The question of work performance is poison for many. Today working time is often the same as the way to the coffee kitchen, the talk in the smoker's corner or at home the clearing out of dishwasher. Peter is annoyed. They must redefine work and eliminate or record creeping leisure activities. Just like at a football match. Everybody can see live if someone works well or is not performing today. Depending on the result the system switches. On the substitutes' bench there is less pay. A kind of paid by use. So, whenever an employee uses the work for leisure time, he pays.

Knocking at the door. Thought crack. His appointment is coming up. New setup, quick jump to the other topic. Their thoughts have been collected in the good old PowerPoint. Their rule of the game: No more than five "charts" per task and person.

Peter uses two of them for introductory questions. They met him at dawn. When he greeted Elisabeth on Monday morning: he saw into a somewhat stunned face. He asked her if everything was okay. "Yes, I do," she explained. Their reasoning was simple and prompted his question: What happens when we press the order button in the web shop? At first glance, it is far from their theme. The second shows like the view through the telephoto lens - surprising closeness.

Peter's charts three and four lead just as far away from her project. His conscience comes out: Does his content mean that he misses the point? Or is it not just the direct way to the goal, which gains benefit? He's cooling off. Displaying logistics more visibly is always allowed. His examples create transparency and hopefully acceptance.

A short time later all charts are on the table. Peter and Larissa cannot believe their eyes and ears. They look at Ethan in amazement. The one who they attributed the least enthusiasm for logistics. He is the one who delivers the best results. He combines known methods in a new way. Questioned. Designs new approaches and sums up: for example, by combining Kanban and Scrum in a new style to improve the planning of logistics in the project.

Scrum he questions right afterwards. His reason: The method applies to existing companies. Suppliers, where only the bosses have the say, encounter cooperative structures at the customer. In the end, his best organization in the project is a virtual one. He brings another example: harmful multitasking. How does Ethan find out if the partners in the network become entangled? It is already difficult to keep your own people from this kind of multitasking.

Furthermore, Ethan compares the product backlog, i.e. the inventory of tasks in the project with the stock. Both are visible to everyone in the Kanban system. Just the tasks for the management in the project. As well as the stock for the purchasing department in the warehouse. Both provide for supplies. Most people know that all. However, many overlook only how close the common understanding is.

In the end Ethan brings the sprint in Scrum together with the principle of baton. He explains this with the Kanban application: The orders in the project and the construction site logistics follow the same basic rule. They follow the pull principle both. Although, there is one weakness for Ethan. He does not entirely trust the principle that the acting persons choose their orders themselves. Despite their obligation to ensure the progress of the project alone. Here, he believes, network and double bottom is required. That's why Ethan is betting is on the sprint backlog in Scrum. In it all features are recorded, which must be ordered for the next sprint. Like the picking in a warehouse. Will only the articles or tasks be stored there which to be delivered shortly. A sprint is for him the 4 by 400 meters or the 4 by 100 meters relay. It is again his thing how many tasks he brings on the way at once. Finally, iteration allows correction and adjustment.

The other tasks, like all the others, are found in the backlog. The duration of a sprint depends on the schedule. Daily updates will do in the chat room of the project. Their advantage: You can write at the same time and save time compared to the meeting. Why? No one needs to hear out the other before he speaks.

"That sounds like a plan," says Peter, "you´ve selected like a buffet from all methods. Well, the proof of the pudding is in the eating. That's good." Peter continues: "However, I think methods or not. Not everybody can be taken away. It is our task to convey the topics in a comprehensible way."

They look at Larissa expectantly. She finds her charts rather bland, almost technocratic. Three goes to Peter. Two to Ethan's. The regulatory circle goes to Peters web shop chart. How does it work and how does it come about? "We will explain the circle control loop over this was", says Larissa. She assigns Peter's refrigerator and supermarket chart to her communication curve. How much communication is necessary to supply shelves and people in everyday life? This complexity is very easy to illustrate in conversation.

Their architectural model is abstract first. However, many have smart homes, phones and so on at home. Means, we live the model already. Probably unconsciously we have the levels process, networking and technology in our mind. She assigns her last two slides to Ethan. Risk assessment and contracts are not far apart.

Finally, they stand in front of Peter's whiteboard. They try to test the assignment and connections. No chart is taken down. Everyone stays in the game. Everyone finds himself again. The different tasks form now a picture. Even if it looks wild at first glance. It would hardly be self-explanatory for third parties. Certainly, a lot of empirical knowledge may cloud the imagination also: because it doesn't look like a solution at first.

They take the term "smart" as a tool. Not in the classic sense of the word, like clever, cunning or fashionable elegance. They use it as the well-known method that helps to describe goals. "Smart" breaks down into its component parts: Specific, measurable, accepted, realistic and time-bound.

For their conversations they are illustrating the digital world with examples from everyday life. Smart Home is specific, if a suction robot works at home. His use is measurable: it is sucked in all corners or not. It is accepted because it is no longer your turn to vacuum. Realistic is because it is feasible. Time-bound, since it stops without any help from anyone. The benefit is clear, you have time for other things.

One question is still open: Why uses everybody digital solutions at home and lose this knowledge on the way to work? Are occur the first media breaks in the mind? Even the ruptures that digitization promises to heal. Are these fractures in the head a symptom or cause of the difficulty with new things? Peter is aware. If they come with ready-made solutions, they are unlikely to survive the initial discussions.

Proposed solutions are like assertions: They provoke resistance. In these cases, the what if question often rotates as a boomerang through the discussion rounds. At home it's different. The woman simply orders the suction robot on the Internet and the discussion is finished.

In working life, the protest really will gets going now. Which ends in work to rule or until the horse being ridden to death. In between they stumble upon catchwords like new work and old school. Why? Because old trails provide security. They are insurance and the right of exist at the same time. Contracts, smooth communication and the familiar are part of it. They cloud the imagination for new things in the best possible way.

The new one sticks in front of them on the white-board. It seems so far away and yet so tempting. What's the next step? Artificial intelligence in the sense of the good old expert systems, datamining & Co? Digital new work provides your project with even more decisions without data. Again, there are more questions than answers.

The toolbox of methods is in front of them. It must be expanded, better sorted and delivered to the people. Connections to everyday life strengthen the imagination. Monitoring and transparency have also part of it. Get the people even more out of the business as usual path!

"We do it like at school when we do our math's. We simplify. Finding the lowest common denominator," sums up Peter. "The path to digital transformation leads via the lowest common denominator of what is possible. That must be determined," he repeats.

Silence in the room. Suddenly, the strategy for digitization is ahead of them. Know what to do if there's nothing to do. It also fits the logistics concept for your project: Determine the lowest common denominator for digitization.

Thunderstorm atmosphere: a consignment belongs into finish, like the football belongs in goal. Otherwise, who likes it when a shipment does not reach its destination? Somebody who blocks results?

The ping echoes in the dark room deafeningly. The mobile phone buzz for the third time. Larissa hears her pulse beating in her ear. No encouraging signs in the early morning. The alarm clock had two hours to go before it had to ring. What happened? She speculates in the semi-darkness First with the little things that make the barrel overflow: The truck didn't make the ferry. Production did not load the crates during the night. The shipment was damaged.

She dreams of the volatile reality in her logistics. To the many shipments, ranging from harmless sapwood to machines with the size of family homes. The faces of production managers and suppliers flash through her mind while she is half asleep. The purchasing department distributes them for the best price, worldwide. "The demands on the best possible logistics and transport organization in projects are high," it roars in her head. "Logistics costs are decisive factors for successful projects. Completely new transport chains and logistics systems must be developed continuously," she hears her professor in grey, years after her past at the university.

Larissa shook up, dozed off again. The alarm clock gives no more time, annoyingly. The dream of half-sleep accompanies her into the bathroom. He ends every time with her fail in the exam. Then she wakes up. Is that a trauma, five years after graduation?

The professor's disturbing image follows her all the way into the bathroom: "Many details, around the core logistical issues, are defined in the design. They have massive influence. Focal points and anchor points are formative examples".

She sees the raised forefinger of the prof, quasi in the mirror. "Many stakeholders tend to underestimate these aspects. In the end, they end up with higher freight rates, additional costs for special transports or invoices for truck waiting times.

Her stomach turns before she gets the first coffee. It was slowly getting light on the screen. The production manager delivers the first mail. "Sorry," it said, "gone stupid." The next is already from the carrier, with the announcement of waiting times. The reason: Her truck stays in front of the factory, it has not been loaded. The next one asks if they need to store or return the box that was on their truck. The offer follows in the annex.

No matter how nebulous the logistics are defined. Everything applies here, only with reversed signs. The right product is in the hall, the wrong crate is on its way. But in the right quantity and in the true quality. Both shipments are in the wrong place at the wrong time. There is no longer any talk of the right costs. The so-called eight "R's", which stand for "Right", turn her stomach.

Larissa stands early in the morning and not only in the shower, with her back to the wall. We need a crash cart. This spontaneously generates two new processes. Doubles the logistics tasks. Two new networks in land transport are being developed. The forces of logistics are now taking effect. Put pressure on her. It is precisely the ability of numerous players to manipulate logistics processes profitably. The everlasting tension, it's up early today. No later than four hours from now, at 9:00 a.m., she will pour pure wine for Ethan.

The first coffee activates further research into the causes. The requirements were clear from the beginning. They were discussed with all relevant actors. Although. The crossed arms of the dispatch manager were warning signs. That could not be overlooked. Dealing with the different interests and groups in the project is simply difficult. To the annoyance of some, they had not used the popular house and farm forwarding agent.

Irrespective of this, it is hard to understand why boxes are left standing and others end up on the wrong truck. The possible combinations are infinitely arbitrary. Is lack of qualification the cause? Hardly likely. Lack of awareness or even omission? At most, the thought accelerates the pulse. Larissa knew that 10 percent of the projects fail due to lack of qualification and motivation of the staff. Honestly, she also embodies the human factor. She would have a hard time absolving herself of it. She is also involved if corporate policy, divisional egoisms and competence wrangling take his effects. She ponders whether the following question is a conspiracy theory or a serious thesis: Who likes it when a shipment does not reach its destination? Who blocks results?

If so, why is that? Are there always people who only watch from the edge of their own plate? Always ready to produce showstoppers somewhere else? Bad communication is without a doubt the number one project killer. Larissa's e-mails show it. Until the new solution is available, many people will certainly be "on the line". Precisely because the clock is ticking: in the project schedule, in the tachograph of the truck or for the rent of the stored crate.

The desired flat hierarchies, set up for rapid communication, do not ensure rapid action in an emergency. Waiting for instructions and orders then gets in the way. But hope dies last. Let's see what can be saved. The follow-up orders to resolve the dilemma must in the pipeline. Today is Saturday.

On the way to the office reaches Larissa at least the ferry on time. She crosses the grey river with busy daydreaming. In them, her problem dissolves into thin air. Project and logistics plan work once again in harmony. The involved people received instructions automatedly on what to do in an emergency. In her dream, it happens that important shipments are equipped with sensors. Digital delivery notes marry crates, shipment tracking systems and truck license plates. Their combination prevents the acknowledgement of the transfer of risk if the chain is not correct. Important alarm messages land immediately on your mobile phone and provide the opportunity to intervene.

Suddenly she and her car are shaken. The ferry stops abruptly. The steel hull slides up the sloping concrete ramp, which serves as a landing stage. A screwed-up docking maneuver. Larissa is back in life. Start the car, drive off.

The dispatch managers' meeting is held every Monday morning. Today the incorrect loading is buzzing around the room. Not that anyone is directly addressed it. None of the present ones puts the other one in the pillory. So, it runs down to the trainee. He just dawdled off his overtime that he needed on Friday evening for the incorrect loading. The dispatch manager mumbles something about a warning. The incident with the new paper padding machine is still not forgotten.

"The fun has gone out of him after he was caught in flagrante delicto: when he packed parcels, filled the cavities and chose larger and larger boxes for the paper padding of the smallest items," says the dispatch manager.

The fact that something is wrong was discovered in Controlling and not in Shipping. The head of purchasing sweeps the subject completely under the carpet with a killer phrase: "Everyone makes mistakes, those who don't make mistakes don't work.

And he adds a spike, in which he exuberantly praises the house and farm forwarding company. Larissa is sitting in the corner with high blood pressure.

Snapped up, she thinks of her part: the trainee, the dispatch manager and everyone else in the company is dealing with the logistics sector. It has always been good and full of ideas in the price and distribution battle. The European logistics market has an annual turnover of almost one billion euros. Germany is the largest market with a share of around 25 percent. So, the actors know their way around. The industry employs more than 2.8 million people. Some are just waiting for the profit, produced by the mistakes of others. Larissa does not see any chance to create a better awareness of this today. Not today. After the shopper came around the corner with his killer phrase.

Larissa asks: "How was the football match at the weekend?"

The reporting starts immediately and patrols through the round. The home team had lost.

Her top comes promptly: "What's it still like with football. If you don't know the running routes, you're not playing along - are you? If the passes are bad and the ball flies to the opponent too often, you lose," she summarizes. "If you apply this to us, it means that the more colleagues know our logistical processes, the better the information and material is passed on - without the shipment ending up at the other party. This also includes trainees and the person who sends them onto the pitch. Logistics is a team game just like football."

The dispatch manager stands up abruptly.

Alarming figures and insights

The Monday round is disbanding. For Larissa is the transport plan for the robots on the agenda. Their march stops abruptly.

In the hallway an employee stands before Ethan and explains sheepishly. The next news that spreads horror: "There are 5,000 euros left for the transports. Everything else has fallen victim to the budget planning."

The transport plan slides to the back. First, money has to be raised. According to the plan, five robots per week are to be loaded onto a ship. Three days later the unloading follows. Accordingly, transport to the port and from the ship to the construction site must be ordered. The dates should be clarified with the manufacturer, i.e. her own holding company.

This puts the key in the hands of the shipping manager. The coherence of the system becomes clear. Larissa needs a transport specification. "*This must be made available for truck and ship transport by the manufacturer's shipping department*". It's to read in a protocol.

Fritz has put his heart and soul into being a shipping manager for thirty years. He is also proud to be back on the works council. That gives him leg room. More and more often he can't keep up. With the ideas and methods of the young people. Managing directors come and resign. Everything is discussed and questioned to the point of vomiting. If he makes a bold claim, they googled at the table and proved the opposite. Now they have founded a company for the new project. Another supposedly brand-new thing. Why? Now they need a transport specification. What for? It's in his head. It is not his first loading of sensitive large components.

"I wasn't there when this was discussed," Fritz plays the ball back flat to Larissa.

Larissa sits in front of Fritz and regrets her comment from the day before. Meanwhile, Fritz throws his self-life wisdom with relish around them. Whenever it becomes concrete.

Reminds her: "After the game is before the game."

She's countering: "Fritz, I don't think there is any specification."

He: "What do you need them for anyway? The Management has to say something about this."

She: "Fritz, the transports have to be planned."

Why question the home and farm transport. He gets along with them very well. Just before Christmas they always think of him. There are things that need to be preserved. At least, in the hustle and bustle of the reorganization he managed to secure the budgets for the transports himself. The project has only received a reminder amount.

He: "Our forwarding agency does that and allow me to point out: The game ends after ninety minutes."

That's the classic and it means trouble. As a precaution, they agree to turn Peter on. At first, he doesn't understand what they want from him. Act as mediator, what a new kind of question from the managers. After the discussion goes around in circles and the sunset approaches, Peter draws the line. At the end, they launch an internal competition for the best transport solution.

Fritz and Larissa are searching for it from now. The purchasing department needs several offers anyway. Two transport variants are considered. One with a transport height of 4.3 meters and one with five meters. The first variant is rejected by production immediately. It requires the partial dismantling of the finished machines. The assembly on the construction site is correspondingly extensive. It was agreed that the feasibility should be checked by means of a route reconnaissance. A route without the usual height restriction of 4.5 meters is to be sought. This means that bridges, railway overhead lines, telephone lines or trees must be bypassed or temporarily removed. With this investigation Larissa is already rid of her 5,000 euros from the budget.

Three weeks later the report is available. A route appears technically and organizationally feasible: From the parent company's plant it leads to a port 30 kilometers away. It has a roll on/roll off loading facility, so that the trucks drive directly onto the ship. Unfortunately, the freighter is only available for intermediate transport to the next ferry port. The direct transport to the port of destination takes too long. The tour does not fit into the schedules that other orders demand. At the end a ferry transports the trucks to the receiving port. From there, the journey continues overland to the construction site - according to the plan.

Fritz calls the usual suspects for his offers. "No problem," was the answer from several corners. The offers are practically finished. Larissa deliberately asks other companies. A little later the first offers come in. There are signs of a debacle. A provider takes the cake with 320,000 euros. Another simply copies his partner's offer and undercuts his prices. He copies the text, just like at school, including typos. The offers of the acquaintances are not much better. They 'll end up with 300,000 euros. Fritz immediately goes under the covers after Larissa presents an offer with 36,000 euros. "This is not serious. That won't work," he grumbles.

Equally frightening figures are shown for transport and pre-advice times. The latter are required by the suppliers to subcontract and obtain authorizations. One needs more, the other less. They offer between 6 and 20 days.

"How can it be, 20 days!" Fritz yells his favorites on the mailbox. "This is not to be given to anyone. How do I explain that the machines will remain in the hall for another 20 days after acceptance by the customer?"

Just as annoying is the range of transport times. The best calculates two days. Of all things, this is Larissa's favorite. The worst ones indicate between 15 and 20 days. Fritz is overcome with the feeling that he is on the losing streak. Presumably his teasing from the meeting with Peter is now catching up with him.

"Don't make a science of it," was his poisonous advice.

If they had followed him, as they always do, they would have been in for around 300,000 euros and three to four weeks' funding. Nevertheless, Larissa must convince him of her carrier. This includes putting it through its paces. He's sitting on the budget. He gives the order.

In the next round of dispatch managers, the plates fly low again. After everyone had understood that the robots had to be dismantled for transport. The production manager lists off overtime, production downtime and delays in the project. Until the embarrassed silence in the round and the numbers in the offers teach him otherwise.

Larissa explains: "The winner is the supplier who has a customer near to the construction site. He provides rear cargo. There are hardly any empty runs. That's how the favorable price is achieved" and adds, "we support them with our control system so that they can reach their connecting transports. Together we can avoid empty runs."

Fritz takes a short breath to rebel but bites his tongue.

"And profit from better prices," Larissa ends.

Fritz basically thinks. Larissa's unusual view of things should not get out of hand. Her thought had never even occurred to him. The reloading of a third party has nothing to do with the own project. Nevertheless, he admits to himself that this approach brings more flexibility. In any case, it is to be expected that the acceptance of the robots by the customer will be delayed. Dead freight and truck waiting times are then unavoidable. Even if the client himself delays the acceptance. He will immediately exert pressure to make up for the alleged loss of time. If they don't have the transports under control, the next claim flies into their faces. The short transit times, the reloading of the transporter and the size of his vehicle fleet is just a good antidote. Fritz does not intend to express his thoughts openly. He will release the budget and order with a lot of "ifs" and "buts". If something goes wrong, it's not his turn anyway. Nevertheless, he must be careful that Larissa doesn't pass him too often on the right side.

Meanwhile Larissa meets real life again; in the form of the project plan. It blows you away. She meets Peter and Ethan in the same room where they recently formulated their path to digitalization. Anger boils high. The pleasant memory of the previous appointment fades away. Larissa reads from the project plan. With difficulty she restrains her sarcastic tone, which is meant for Peter and quickly and fluently turns into a bitchy one. The paragraphs she reads out feel like ankle cuffs. Suspicion springs up. She doubts whether they are really in the same boat.

"The manufacturer has the authority to give instructions at the construction site. In his absence, the executing installation company. This includes the crane and transport work as well as all processes that ensure smooth progress on the construction site".

And further: "A construction site diary must be kept. Furthermore, a daily site meeting must be held. All the points must be recorded in writing and countersigned by the manufacturer, the representative of the project company, the assembly company and the transport and crane company.

Ethan recoups the cost of the daily construction meetings. Can't this exchange be organized differently? For example, via chat? Peter ponders the strategy again. He wishes modern methods in logistics management. How can this be done? Meanwhile, Larissa gets the impression that the two are elsewhere with their thoughts. She brings them back without further ado, onto the carpet:

"This means we are out as a project company! We are the vicarious agents of the suppliers and the customer. Our task, the service as a scapegoat," she summarizes and continues moaning, "if everything goes well, we are asked again and again if a project company is needed at all. If anything goes wrong, we're grilled. No matter who makes the claim!"

Larissa continues: "The logistical valley is the construction site. And it is precisely here each coordinates its logistical tasks supplier independently. This is to be explained by the Public Procurement and

Contract Regulations. Logistics sees as a contractual accessory obligation of the construction contract. It falls within the responsibility of the respective contractor. So as a project company we are hanging in the air. Our contractual partner is Virtuell.AN. This means the project company is subordinate to the site manager of Virtuell.AN. Not to mention the fact that we also have no direct access to the logistics of the suppliers. Sure, they know their products. However, the limits are set by the conditions on the construction site. Depending on the supplier, the tasks of construction site logistics change. Individual heavy transports must be planned. Other parts are to be assembled in principle from the truck. Many small parts create mass volume."

Larissa now talks into a rage herself: "Further straitjackets will delivered to us with the agreement of the Incoterms DAP delivered at place. The suppliers fulfil their mission if they make the trucks available for unloading. The subsequent work is again regulated in separate contracts with the installation companies. The construction site logistics of Virtuell.AN is responsible for unloading. Storage included, if one of them is not ready. The suppliers give their transport orders to third parties. They come when they want and become the drivers of construction site logistics: I have counted more than 60 logistics service providers. This is the result of your purchasing department if they leave the logistics to each supplier. Your steel construction company, for example, is using their House and Farm delivery service."

Larissa writes on the flipchart: "First service provider". "This company outsources the transport to another trucking company", she explains: "Second service provider". "Another trucking company is transporting the devices: Number three. Although it is equipped with own vehicles, they still decided to use two subcontractors for the job". Service providers four and five land on the flipchart.

"The example shows only five of the 60 logistics service providers. Everyone is involved in the project with their organizations and interests. Many are interdependent. Like the transporter from the packer or the shipping departments from the goods receipt of the next. The tasks are spread over many shoulders. A huge network! How long does it take to do something similar on a social network?"

Larissa finishes her picture on the flipchart. Hierarchies appear and the white spots on the map increase. All you can hear in the room is the squeaking of the pen on the paper. Peter feels as he often does: You think things are solved and the boomerang comes back faster than expected. The system is simply robust and new things are leveraged. The keepers simply continue to work as before.

"Okay, thanks Larissa", he says, "that's enough for today. I don't think that's our final predicament."

Nod in agreement from Larissa.

"All right, or not, I'll see you in the morning", Peter ends the day.

Endless footcuffs and straitjackets:

Shortly after the start of the day it catch up with that what Peter feared the evening before. "Good morning", Larissa wishes them all, "I appear with three examples! They all fit the pattern: as far as I can see show they further horror scenarios".

"Wait a minute," interrupts Ethan, who was strangely introverted in the last session, "if this goes on just as it did last night, then I wonder what roles are intended for the project company? Are we customer buffer, keeper alibi of Virtual.AN, the bodyguard for liabilities or all in one, Peter?"

Oh, thinks Larissa. She has rarely seen Ethan so clearly. Otherwise, he'll listen before he gets started. Probably he heard enough yesterday.

"If Fritz doesn't come out with his budget for the robot transports, we're up against the wall!" Ethan's had enough for now.

"That's exactly how my examples fit," Larissa seizes the moment, "may I?" Consenting nod at Peter. Kind of an "oh, no" move on Ethan.

"The first concerns the steel construction sections. To be installed in the foundation. The project plan says: The delivery and transport plan must be agreed in detail with the executing construction company. The project company is responsible for determining and monitoring the time schedule. That puts us right back in the middle." And further: "The installation of the sections is to be documented in writing and with pictures, as well as to be made available to the customer in digital form after completion of the work".

Larissa continues reading without a break: "Any structural changes to the concrete structure must be reported in writing. During concrete curing, care must be taken to ensure that the corresponding values are maintained. These are to be verified by measurement reports. If the concrete quality is too low or is installed within the curing days, is this the responsibility of the project company. After completion of the concrete work, the project company must prepare a levelling report per section and make it available to the customer. The earthing of the sections must be carried out professionally by a local electrical and lightning protection company and measured in accordance with the customer's lightning protection guidelines. The measurement reports must be submitted to the client one month before the start of the next construction phase and approved by the client", Larissa ends.

"Then at least I am the construction, project and logistics manager for the sections. That's great. The customer gets everything from one source," Ethan thinks.

"The second example", Larissa is consciously ignoring Ethan. The problems belong on the table once and for all. Now was the opportunity. "It concerns the main crane for the construction of the steel structure. As well as the conclusion of the crane contracts for the installation of the robots, including sufficient auxiliary cranes for unloading, loading and handling in the port of departure and reception," Larissa lists.

"The requirement profile of the main crane must be defined together with the supplier. A second main crane with an auxiliary crane shall be provided in co-ordination. Periods of bad weather must be compensated. The project company will ensure that the crane company contracted covers enough hook load insurance. Proof amounting to 2.5 to 3.0 million euros must be submitted. Crane operators must provide evidence of their training. The project company ensures that an English-speaking site manager is present on the construction site every day. The crane drivers are trained in English to the extent that they do not hinder communication on the construction site.

Larissa now reads a little louder: "The type of crane for loading and unloading, the ships and handling in the ports must be agreed with the manufacturer and approved by him. The project company must draw up a site plan for storage in the port of destination. This must be agreed with the manufacturer. The same applies to the material that is stored with the facilities in the port of destination. The storage area in the port must be protected against access by third parties. A security service is to be commissioned for "round-the-clock" surveillance. Furthermore, the plants must be secured against storms. Winter protection may be necessary (sleet, hail, rain). A capacitor must be provided for the storage period in order to protect the components against moisture occurring in the packaging. An adequate power supply must be provided. The project company will prepare photographic documentation for all shipments. Any transport damage must be reported immediately to the manufacturer. The project company bears the costs. The amount of the transport insurance shall be agreed with the manufacturer. Larissa leans back and looks over the edge of the project plan into the round.

"Someone's got it all sorted," rumble Ethan, "all risks and anything dubious off to the project company. After that we are now carrier, photographer and payer. I don't want to speculate. Fortunately, most of it - by pure coincidence - is obsolete now. With the solution about the ferry that Larissa has worked out. Or do you think Fritz and his friends are still holding a boomerang?"

"What I ask myself", Larissa continues, "there is no longer a word here about the modes of the transport and lifting. The equipment is missing that can be used to lift and move the components in the port, on the construction site or for securing the load. They represent a not inconsiderable value and creates own transport processes, with all cost and risks. Including the return of the empties. Apart from the fact that the values require tracking by sensor technology and telematics, as does the corresponding insurance. So far we've only been able to produce a bank guarantee."

"Is this a trap now," Ethan asks, "or I am already seeing ghosts? Does someone intend to literally hang us in the air at some point? If so, why? If only one factor changes in any direction. Like missing measurement reports, expertise's or a release, then it is not only the logistics. In order to reanimate the processes. I talk to many actors who are quickly in unpacking their interests; while I stand with my back to the wall.

Peter is silent so far. Now, he is no longer so sure whether the project company was a good idea. In fact, it appears someone has been picked the cherries. As managing director of both companies, he is nicely sitting between the chairs.

"My third example," Larissa replies, "goes a little in that direction. On the one hand, the notes and appointments are more than useful. Nevertheless, they also support Ethan's hunch."

At lunch time they evaluate the notes which Larissa presents for her third example. "It concerns the devices. With their length of 27 meters, a height of seven meters and a width of two meters, they display remarkable house numbers," says Larissa. "Each one weighs 50 tons."

Like a lawyer reading out a will, she reads out the notes: "Conversation of the 15th of the month: About load securing, transport procedure and deadlines, we have discussed the two possible variants: firstly, the sloping position, secondly, the lying position on the truck.

The transport height of the trailers is 30 centimeters. They're pull-out low bed trailers. In an inclined position they are a maximum of four meters high. Together with the trailer it´s results in a transport height of 4.30 meters. Anything beyond means police escort along the entire route and prior route reconnaissance. The reason: the maximum clear height of the road bridges is 4.5 meters. It should be noted that the height is reduced due to new road surfaces sometimes. In this case, alternative routes must be worked out. Factors that increase costs and transport risks.

Attachment points must be provided for tipping, loading and unloading. The tilting process requires two gantry cranes or hoists with a minimum lifting capacity of 25 tons. The same applies to the lifting gear. For the construction site, two mobile cranes with the appropriate lifting capacity and a jib length of five meters are to be provided.

A crane operator and three employees are provided by the manufacturer for loading. The truck driver is responsible for securing the load. The manufacturer designs and manufactures the corresponding transport frames. It is his responsibility to check that the goods are in a safe condition for loading. The attachments as well as the boxes for two fixtures are loaded onto a third semi-trailer. A total of three trucks in a convoy with two fixtures.

Loading takes place in the first and second shift. If, in exceptional cases, the third is required, the truck drivers will coordinate their work in good time and directly with the responsible staff here on site (standby).

With the original position of the lifting eyes, the height of 4.3 meters is exceeded. For this reason, two lifting eyes are attached laterally outside the contour line. The design department believes this to be feasible. The position of the remaining attach-ments is important for maintaining the transport height. Others are very likely to be damaged due to the load securing measures (tie-down lashing and welding). These are dismantled, transported in addi-tional boxes and reassembled on site.

For the "diagonal" variant, daytime travel with a permanent permit is conceivable. The lying alterna-tive is, due to its width, feasible with individual ap-proval and only after 22.00 hrs in night-time driving. The total transport time results from the drivers' driv-ing and rest periods.

Basic procedure: Over a period of eight weeks, four fixtures shall be delivered each week. The con-struction site announces the final starting time. Two devices are to be transported, as described, with three vehicles each. Loading is on Monday and Tuesday morning for arrival on Wednesday and Thursday. It will be unloaded immediately. Empty transport frames are loaded. The returns are not subject to approval, so that the weekend driving ban remains unaffected. Accordingly, the trucks are back on Friday and Saturday evening.

The disposition of the transports, i.e. the exact number as well as the loading and unloading times are announced each Thursday by email for the coming week. Friday remains as a reserve, as does the deployment of a second driver. The latter reduces waiting times due to the driving time regulations. Signed Peter", Larissa ends her monologue. And asks in surprise, "That's not you, Peter, is it? That's a really viable plan!"

"Thanks for the flowers," Peter replies, "Fritz wished a working student some time ago. I think his neighbor's son's is called Peter and he was active here during the holidays."

"But no student works this out alone," says Ethan, "there were more involved. This is a feasibility study, with significant implications."

"Anyway, this is a ray of hope in the whole mix", Larissa comments, "regardless of that; I don't know how you see it. I mean:

Nothing works anymore: in the current project the horse has bolted; more and more conflicting goals are coming to light.

We even run the risk and drive with the project company to the wall. All the responsibilities and traps they've cobbled together. They leave us as lame duck standing in the rain without any possibility to act. We may put out the fires and take responsibility for them, but we may not treat the causes."

"It seems to me that it's not only the project's logistics felled off the wagon in the course of the project development," curses Ethan, "how do we solve all the knots? With this imbalance, complexity increases with the number of bypasses for ad hoc solutions. Not only the costs endanger the success of the project. The boat is in danger of capsizing. To correct the course, quick action is required before everyone deflects to the other side."

"I agree," Peter tries to escape, "but what will be gained, if we dissolve the project company. The issues remain. Just under the carpet, like before. As always, new things create resistance, with the maintainer and guardians. That's why the existing system is so robust. Peter continues his monologue: "As the saying goes: with the organization and not against it will something performed, for example logistics. If projects fail, it is often not the professional or technical area at all, but rather the interpersonal and communicative area. As I said, logistics serves as an example here. You don't hear about them in Monday meetings, but in direct conversation and in well-dosed confrontation. He breathed deeply: "Without this workup, we will gain no insights. Even if, they are crass and sobering at first like here. It was predictable that Fritz will go on the barricades. Until now, we have turned over many stones in all areas to optimize the company. Except for the logistics. This is the last bastion."

"Is that the role of the project company?" Ethan asks.

"Definitely an important one," Peter replies, "we're already getting some movement in the matter. This was shown by the rivality to transport the robots."

"What do you mean?" Ethan asks.

Peter answers the question indirectly: "We have a conflict of goals here. One part insists on his known supplier, the next on the cheapest one."

"It's a common saying, if you buy cheap, you pay twice," Larissa replies, "and anyone whose price you squeeze down to the last cent will get their money back at the next opportunity.

"It's obvious," Ethan interrupts, "Conflicts of interest are everywhere in life. The balance between leisure and work, family and friends. Working less becomes a conflict of objectives if this means a drop-in income. Higher wages lead to the dilemma of making more profits in the company.

"Exactly Ethan," Larissa agrees with him, "resolving conflicts of interest is a daily business for us. Sometimes it requires the squaring of the circle. Synergies must be used, and cargo packages must be bundled. Reduce prices while remaining flexible. Save on packaging, but do not risk transport damage. Do not oversize them so that transport costs do not increase. The purchasing department buys additional quantities at favorable prices and increases storage costs. The examples can be continued at will." Larissa turns to the whiteboard and asks, "do we have the time?"

"We'll take them," Peter says. "Ethan, what do you think?"

"It's almost dark and I'm hungry," Ethan thinks.

"Again, okay then we'll order rolls again," Peter replies.

"Well, let's yell at them," Ethan replies, "I think logistics is going to be my new passion." And rubbing his non-existent stomach.

Larissa is painting. The sketch shows an octagon. She gives the corners the concepts of redundancy and efficiency. This is followed by standardization and responsiveness. The third pair consists of well-known and cheapest providers. Corner seven and eight designates them as central and decentralized.

She explains: "I see redundancy as opposed to efficiency. For me, the latter is profitability. It means achieve the best possible result with as little effort as possible. Standardization speaks against responsiveness, at least for initial processes. Central and decentralized are always counterpoints. Just like the classic; the choice between the well-known and the cheapest provider. The case has just gone over our stage. I think Fritz bears it us after." Larissa continues: "Normal is actually the opposite. The budget always says yes to the best offer. The procurement department feels the same. Why the cheapest led in our case almost to a scandal remains a mystery. I would understand if the cheapest is not a blank slate. If is, it becomes a torture. In our case the alarm lamps light up for a different reason."

"Well, Fritz combines acquaintance with reliability and reliable with tried and tested", Peter shows understanding, "a secure process is for him, if he is as little occupied with it as possible. If somebody still twitches at the end, he modestly reminds the purchasing department that customer payments are often dependent on successful transport. No one contradicts him then. The door for the cheapest one closes at the latest when he adds that cash flow is without a question one of the most important aspects in a business relationship.

"Oh well, another great argument from the Murder and Manslaughter Division. Fritz also knows it is the information that triggers the flow of materials and the right flow of information triggers the flow of money," remarks Larissa, "sometimes is requested too much information. And these are then of varying, often poor quality. Nevertheless," Larissa continues, "our little method requires calibration." She draws several triangles in the octagon.

The buns stop her. Elisabeth stands in front of the glass door and swings the tray.

"Logistics again?" she asks in disbelief as she enters. "Is this going to be our new core business?"

"Yes of course," Peter replies, "the most people just don't know it yet."

After the meal they break up the round and arrange to meet for the next afternoon. Everyone leaves the room introverted. Nobody feels swing and good mood, but also no concrete block on the leg.

"Time-out": On the quality of personnel and thus on organizational development; is it allowed to compare employee-employer relationship with the life cycles of products?

Back in his office, Peter feels trapped. Captivated by logistics, project and personnel. He turns on his heels. Walked into the coffee room. On the way to the double espresso, the employees who are still there today greet him. Others encounters him as images in his head: Ethan, Fritz, Larissa, the trainee, the student and Elisabeth.

He tries to sort his thoughts with abstract thinking. Certainly, nobody would think of using Formula 1 professionals in the German Football League. A logistician with expertise from the pharmaceutical sector will probably feel the same when he is threatened involved in a large-scale plant project. Larissa would be under stretched in reception, Elisabeth would be overstretched in the project. Her common sense can only be of limited help there.

Peter continues to deliberately think in abstract terms and asks himself: Is the quality of personnel in logistics under- or overestimated? A truck is rarely delayed because the driver has forgotten how to steer it. It is more likely that customers, suppliers, their own scheduling, driving times or other road users exert their influence. In other words, all players in the logistics system. Peter is aware that the ideal employee or employees do not exist. Rather like in real life, there are different types. How can the targets be better implemented in the company's network from this aspect?

He speaks a note on his mobile phone: "First indent: If logistics aims, for example, at cost leadership, standardization and capacity utilization, then employees are required who accept instructions and implement them reliably. They are receptive to financial incentive and routine. Actively shaping a logistics system seems to be less her motive".

Peter continues to dictate: "Second indent: If logistics is aimed at specific, non-flat-rate and adaptable solutions, employees with expertise are needed in my opinion. The willingness to take responsibility and initiative is her thing as well as the desire for self-development. They are questioning instructions. Demand more flexibility. Are less motivated by material incentives. They claim freedom for themselves by deciding and acting independently. They have a strong interest in actively designing logistics systems. Their professional development is important for them." Peter presses "Stop" and puts his cell phone back in his pocket.

Back in his office, he draws the examples as antipoles on his whiteboard. It´s clear between the North and South Pole is much more. The following case comes to his mind again: the carrier with the best price has an authoritarian, "patriarchal" management style. The boss decides alone. The latter meets a supplier where the focus is on the scope of responsibility and action as well as local decisions. The employees are used to cooperative leadership. How do the teams of both houses work together? When the bosses live on different poles? Who moderates and navigates between them? Likely, notes Peter; his project manager.

Several questions result simultaneously: To what extent is the logistics process dependent on the management style of the respective partners? Do complex employee types generate the desired dynamics? Or is it more likely that frictional losses will occur?

Peter notes opposites: independent work here, subordinate work there. Personal responsibility and holistic thinking in one place, responsibility alone at the top elsewhere. The same applies to functional thinking. Scope for action yes and no. The stress fields are formed itself automatically. It would surprise him, if they were to pay attention to such contradictions in the course of clarifying the mission. In the event of an incident, the mechanisms of the classical hierarchy always work safely. So to say free to the door and without advance order. The cases end up on his table. He notes an idea: In the future, a personnel concept will be requested with the invitation to tender. The latter does not only ask for the CVs of the project staff, but also asks for the concept of personnel management and development.

The Task seems to be easier at virtual companies. Like their project company.   They bring companies with agreements for a partnership together. They will continue to exist until the targets are achieved. The required teams meet for a specific challenge the personal and professional requirements. Peter notes one example: "In the past, forwarding agencies were always hierarchically structured. Shipowners and port companies appeared in the same way. However, they join forces to handle a transport. Carriers, shipping companies or airlines work together under the umbrella of a forwarding agency. If the transport is completed, the virtual company disappears again until to the next operation.

A little later Peter ends up on his way home in a traffic jam. Time to think ahead. He asks himself a moral question: Is it permissible to compare employment relationships with the life cycles of products?

Applies to them not the same as a life span? Fritz, for example, belongs to the inventory. He is firmly embedded. Larissa is new, works on a project basis and is less connected to the company. She likes presumably rather interesting projects than continuity. Appreciates Peter. Fritz he counts with all his qualities among the keepers. If he doesn't like something, he hits the brakes. In return Fritz is enthusiastic about his roles in shipping and in the works council. It's promoted him to a kind of informal pack leader between purchasing and production. Obvious defeats, such as in the competition for transport prices, will not please him. It is more like biting the bullet in public. It is undermined his position.

Lost in thought saw Peter, that the fourth green phase at the same traffic light slipped through for him. Back in the present he steps on the brakes. He sees now the rolling advertising banner on the street corner with full consciousness. The product advertising of the banner leads Peter back to the initial question: Is it permitted to compare product life cycles and employment relationships?

If yes, then the idea is at the beginning: develop products or hire employees. Peter compares the second phase of innovation, in which the products are created, with the search and selection of employees. This ends with the entry into the market. Accordingly, the new colleague has his first working day. His fame is initially as low as his image and trust. In the familiarization phase you will feel your way around. Start-up losses must be calculated. With the growth phase, the employee achieves increasing prominence, a better image and the first profits with his services. Sound the horn behind Peter points to the green traffic light in front of him. He's drives on so late that the honker doesn't make it again. At the next corner he stands again.

He picks up his mobile phone and speaks a voice note: "The 'return of investment' occurs, if the costs of the innovation and introduction phase are offset by profits. Afterwards employees or products generate net profits for the company. He gains further experience in positive and negative ways. At some point he is more skillful, and the everyday life is going over to routine. Habits in working life seem most comparable to the saturation of products on the market," dictates Peter. He presses the stop button. Drives on. Brakes sharply. Types the button and say: "The decline is accompanied by the lamentation of the circumstances. Dissatisfaction arises or will be created. This means the beginning of the end. In the worst case, the number of sick days increases. The willingness to perform decreases and error costs increase. At the end of it is the termination. Depending on how that happens, it can turn into lawsuits. Whether it is right or not is irrelevant. It means efforts for many. In any case more diseases are likely from then on."

Two crossings later is calculating Peter in his head: A project employee would like to receive 60,000 euros a year. To the salary he adds personnel follow-up costs of 20 percent, making 72,000 euros. For the selection they use a recruitment agency. In such cases it takes over the tasks of the personnel department. Searches and job interviews take three months or more quickly. Until the final employment contract is signed. The costs for the company add up, plus 10,000 euros to a total of 82,000 euros. From the first day of work, the employee is trained for three months by an experienced colleague. He is the second man in the projects. Peter rates the induction by the workmate at 60 hours per month. Over the period he calculates: 180 teaching hours, 50 euros each equals 9,000 euros. The sum increases to 91,000 euros.

In the first year, a salary of 60,000 euros is paid, quickly leading to total costs of almost 100,000 euros. Peter tries his hand at the breakeven: They charge the customer a maximum of 100 euros per hour. The first 480 are not chargeable, because the customer sees the incorporation integrated in the prices. That leaves 1,120 of the approximately 1,600 hours that an employee works per year. The 100,000 euros are covered after 1,000 hours. The breakeven occurs at the beginning of the twelfth month of employment.

Peter sums up. With a normal project duration of two years, there is little time for new employees to earn their money for the employer. However, without that it does not work. If there are no orders in the third year, profits are quickly lost. Furthermore, if the financial reserves in the company are used up, the rights in the employment contract still apply. One thing is then certain: resistance when it comes to cutting salaries. The desire for more pay remains unchanged. No matter what the situation is. It is no wonder that companies try to reduce risks through virtual companies and fixed-term contracts.

At home after dinner splashes a predictable love movie on television. His wife loves her. Peter continues to think about it: for many people is important; the structures first, then the processes. Her structure is based on task and job descriptions which cements the framework. The necessary authority of the employees is embedded in it. Hierarchies are oriented towards the top. Employees orientate themselves by this. They are trained for this. Management positions are filled in the same way. Everyone works in their own area of responsibility. Functional thinking is in the foreground. The willingness of the individual to communicate and cooperate moves within the framework of instructions. In extreme cases, head down and deliver applies.

Peter is looking for a note.

His wife looks at him and her look asks, "Are you working?"

He's taking notes. A shaking head on the other side of the sofa. How does it work when the partner, customer and supplier networks are organized similar? How many other organizational patterns emerge in a project? Are there more virtual companies in it?

Is there part more the networking and professional presentation? What happens to the seemingly unforeseen? Is that beyond the scope?

Peter gets his laptop and writes down a fictitious example: Like a bolt from the blue 30 crates are stuck in customs in the importing country. It is easy to see that advance warnings about new regulations on the treatment of wood packaging were overheard. For the project the horse has bolted. In reasons of cost and time, the company has waived at network and double ground. The formal Organisation jumps therefore too short.

No one is helping in this case. The project and logistics management has clarified the successive and interdependent tasks for the undisturbed course of events. Which control the distribution of information in the network and trigger the material flow in the first place. Anticipating the apparently unforeseen requires experience and the courage to make decisions. This includes a high communication culture, which in turn does not belittle or dismiss negative forecasts.

Meanwhile Peter is spinning in circles. Again, he lands with the quality of the staff. The courage to make decisions, communication and team spirit will be affirmed by everyone in the job interview. Nevertheless, in an emergency the formal organizations leave the back doors open for him. They enable also the search of troubles only at any others. By pointing out its responsibilities and presenting its own tasks, which cannot be depart from. For Peter are these human reactions: If somebody wants to acquit themselves from it. He should think to those who live in glass houses and try to throw stones. For Peter these are reasons which speaks for virtual companies. It´s a management method for him. Mobile task forces are also part of this. The preparation alone is based on prevention. Precisely the avoidance of operations in an emergency. They work independently of existing structures and thus help her. If several task forces are networked in the business process, is a modular organization live. The focus is process orientation. Coordination becomes a management task.

In the love film the expected final scene takes place. The end is coming.

Act Three

Choreography or consolidation. The conflicting goals of logistics must be resolved.

A few kilometers further on sits Ethan completely baffled in his apartment. He can't get the puzzle together. How can the parts be brought into line with the logistics spectacles? In his project company, 18 people are currently employed with the project. Six suppliers have been identified, including the parent company. They each bring in 18 employees. Several other logistics service providers have to be determined which they need for pre-carriage, main carriage and on-carriage. Ethan assumes ten for better arithmetic. Which will be active again with 18 employees.

His example shows 17 companies. The number of people who work - even if only partially - for his project amounts to 306 in his calculation, 17 times 18 people. If everyone networks with everyone else, 93,330 communication connections will result. It is the old bills that they overtake again in communication. Sure, not all wires will glow, but how does the individual know when, why and to what is to communicate? Breaks in information flow are to be expected. For logistics, these fractures mean that the baton falls. The figures can be easily calculated for each project. If the figures are used as eye-catching, they show the direction of organizational development.

They illustrate that the flow of information via mobile phone or e-mail alone cannot be managed. They also show that very few people will get to know each other personally. They remain unknown beings in the project. Even if, as in the social networks, they become visible with their personal profiles.

Ethan understands such considerations are difficult during project development. The early phase is characterized by competition and tendering. Afterwards follows the order clarification. But, why do projects fail? According to his knowledge, the figures for the damage caused by faulty project work are in the two to three-digit billion range. Error costs are seldom an issue in contract negotiations, apart from the insurance issue. Afterwards are supplements or claims the means of choice. Ethan is still going on with his puzzle. Many parts do not yet fit completely. Although the findings are on the table.

His experience with the frequent changes of personnel at the executive and the project manager level gets in the way. After that, it is the managers, which fresh from university controls sub-projects worth millions. The bidding and awarding procedures, which virtually provoke supplements and claims, are always in Ethan's way. In addition, there are delays, budget overruns and seemingly unforeseeable bottlenecks that alternate time and again.

Optimization approaches threaten to fail in such mixed situations. There is a lack of data and experience knowledge for prevention. The same applies to forecasts by simulation. Before information's are missing. During the project they are maintained analogously, if at all, or kept under lock and key. The white spots on the data map are correspondingly large.

However, the knowledge of the individual is imperfect. It's not the first time Ethan has had this insight sitting on his sofa. He writes a "help me mail": His invitation for the next meeting with Peter and Larissa.

This meeting is controversial. After Ethan has started the others follow up with their worries and needs. For Peter, it feels like a maelstrom is pulling him down. They are on a good way to set checkmate themselves, he fears. The silhouette "nothing goes" appears in the atmospheric sky of the discussion. "When is it time to draw up a consolidation plan to get logistics back on track," asks Peter.

"Why, has bankruptcy occurred?" replies Larissa.

"No, it's just a possibility in a conflict situation. Of course, what we are gathering here is heavy ballast for the project. But for me is it also part of the analysis. We describe our demands. It is made visible by the bad weather atmosphere that prevails in the room today," explains Peter. "It doesn't help to throw ballast overboard. This does not turn us into a speedboat and we also get into a spin. However, what we know is a great deal. The skids are part of it, okay. In any case, we make progress in transparency."

Peter turns to the whiteboard and writes: "What we have" and in indents below:
- Analysis of the existing system is possible.
- Making logistics systems more visible, in progress.
- A more centralized control of material and information flows is on the way.
- Specify transport requirements, in progress.

- Comparing storage and transport variants are clearer to everyone now.
- Market inquiries and selection of logistics service providers, in case of doubt in the competition for the best solution.
- Bundling of logistics service providers and thus the reduction of interfaces, is recognized and addressed.

The organization in the project:
- Implementation of a unit to control the logistics service providers used.

To relieve project participants of logistics tasks at all levels:

- Creation of a visual dashboard for tracking individual shipments.
- Development and expansion of a logistics supplier network in the greater area of the construction site.
- Review of the previous transports.
- Continuous determination of logistics costs and creation of cost transparency
- Documentation of project findings for the benefit of subsequent projects.

"This looks like a script," Ethan comments somewhat smugly, "but you don't have another actor on board yet. At most the actors behind the scenes, who make us fight against wind and rain on stage. Certainly, with this a new guideline for the operational implementation is possible. But how do we get everyone to follow that?"

"Maybe the conflicting targets in logistics will help us. Everyone is caught up in this dichotomy; and not only in logistics. If we nominated these dilemmas, we create attention for us by the colleagues. Last time we did not finish with our new method. You remember the eight conflicting goals. They are all connected and keep pushing us into a dilemma. The octagon went over into triangles. They help us to compensate the dichotomy. What do you think? Should we continue to work out the method and try it out?"

"Okay! A kind of life belt," Ethan thinks aloud, "let's try it. We prepare a workshop with Fritz and colleagues. Then we'll have the right candidates at the table."

"Great, let's go," Peter replies.

Two weeks later Fritz is sitting at the table. "Well, what have you come up with now?" he greets the group.

Crossed arms signal skepticism. Eckard, head of purchasing, is there as well as the student from the neighborhood. This time he works in the construction department during the semester break. The sales manager is also present.

Fritz greets him with a friendly greeting: "What brings you here, have you already successfully scared off all the customers today?"

Larissa wonders if Eckard is acting as bodyguard for Fritz. The sales manager has appeared presumably as Peter's listening post. He sought the wideness at the last moment, with a rather strange excuse. At the very least, it secures him the position of the conciliator when the mood escalates.

Ethan's going on. "Good morning, everyone. We have been dealing a lot with the logistics in our project recently. Many thoughts go through our heads. They are close to our hearts and therefore we have the desire to share and discuss them with you. Larissa has developed a kind of methodology, which serves us a little as a guide. We need your opinion. The method is new and hopefully it will help us for a better understanding of many issues and dilemmas. Is that okay for you?"

"Well then, we'll be curious," answers Fritz slightly pompously.

"Larissa, it's your turn," Ethan asks her.

As before, Larissa records her octagon with the conflicting goals.

About the well-known and cheapest supplier Eckard comments: "I always say, if you buy cheap, you buy twice."

"That's nothing new," replies Fritz. "Just as central and decentralized, it´s driving the sow through the village again. We also always work with network and double bottom. If you combine that with redundancy."

"So how do you work economically, i.e. efficiently?", the student from the neighborhood asks.

"After the horse has already left the barn, nobody will ask about it. Save what can be saved is then right at the top of the agenda. I work effectively in this moment. What do you think would I hear if my answer is: why you told me to be efficient? Besides, in preliminary planning is neither time nor money for plan B. Just the whistling in the woods can be heard from those who always demand it at the green table," Fritz says to his neighbor son.

"That's why I'd like it if we could create a solution pattern," Larissa interjects, "I'll show you what I mean." Her pen squeaks on the flipchart again between the cheapest known provider and redundancy to the triangle.

"Why like that?" Larissa asks into the round.

"You are looking for a corrective," the student replies, "an indicator of the necessary compromise a balance between opposites.

Silence in the room, amazed looks. *He didn't fall on his head; my neighbor* thinks Fritz.

"Exactly", Larissa continues, "no professional team competes in football without a passably staffed substitutes' bench. In this case redundancy is useful. For us, this means, we have at least two or more service providers for the same task in the project. Known, unknown or recommended ones are considered equally, redundantly. Who makes it into the squad, onto the substitutes' bench or into the starting eleven depends on several factors: We evaluate prices, default risks, bid exclusions and our coordination efforts. The game is played with open cards. If the competition is fair, it gives the project wings, just like in football."

"That sounds simple," says Eckard, "for most companies, the awarding process involves a tender or at least the comparison of three offers. More is needed here. The demands request, called "BANF", is usually sent to us. We check the market and obtain quotations. As already mentioned, the "BANF" is supplemented, depending on its scope, by a specification. The procedure is independent. If you have already worked with the provider or not is irrelevant. In case of doubt, we use cost benefit analysis to minimize the subjective character of the evaluation. In rare cases several suppliers are commissioned, which we then control via call-off orders. If I say it in your words Larissa: We rarely work with a spare bench. The comparison with golf or tennis is might be the better one. Your example does not fit in my opinion," Eckard concludes his speech.

"Okay, if the player drops out, the match is lost. Still, you always have several rackets or something with you in case one breaks. This is your choice for redundancy. Accordingly, I would ask where redundancy is possible and up to what point. This is where the 'point-of-no-return' must be determined," the student answers.

"I guess you have an answer for everything," Eckard replies dryly.

"Well worked out," shouts Larissa.

"Hold your horses. The dilemma between redundancy and efficiency follows on foot. You have just asked about it," Fritz continues, "doubts remain: if we buy things twice, then it is effective because both serve the goal. It's not efficient. What do you need a second transport systems? If the project goals can be achieved with one of them? Not to mention that it's hard to argue when we're developing the project or calculating bids."

Larissa replies:

"Every logistician on the project will crank up plan B in his head when he finishes plan A, won't he?"

"Yes, of course" mumbles Fritz.

"I mean, you will timbering your double bottom with it or hang up the net for the freestyle in the trapeze," Larissa continues. Ethan imagines the swaying circus tent. Sees Fritz doing the "Salto mortale".

"The question is, what is if not?" adds Larissa, "in my opinion, the next set screw is called reactivity or switching game to stay with football." Larissa's pen squeaks and pulls the next triangle together.

"Admittedly, it depends on the propensity for trans-formation. For this reason, the plan B and C is not only in the drawer. Ideally, should it be trained."

Ethan objects: "Responsiveness requires activa-tion and coordination first, as well as a concrete case. Only then can the result be assessed at all. It´s difficult to calculate as a preventive measure in Plan B or C and especially in the planning phase, isn't it?"

"Please take our robots as examples. The cus-tomer does not take they on time. Ordered ship-ments are postponed, several times. When he finally wants, agreed times for advance notice are obso-lete. Afterwards the lack of understand follows in large steps if the special trucks are not immediately in the yard. Additional costs are rejected anyway", Larissa answers a little bit snotty. "I remind the email which you sent me last time just before midnight."

"Why, what did it say?" Fitz asks with relish.

"Larissa, find a new forwarder," growls Ethan.

Laughter at the end of the table. "That was a great idea. You wanted to change the forwarder who is also the holder of the transport permit. This will cost you two to three weeks. After you have found and commissioned the new one. This is tantamount to a refusal to play, with one three to zero for the others," Fritz continues to throw salt in the wound.

"Anyway," Larissa squeezes herself in again, "it's definitely a fitting example of the point-of-no-return. By the way, your friends would probably have lost the game before kick-off. Perhaps we can settle on a draw here and move on to the next item."

General agreement.

"In my opinion, standardization stands in the way of reaction," she explains, "as mentioned, it depends on the ability to change over. While standardization aims at the unification of dimensions, types, procedures, structures and others".

"But that's exactly what creates the possibility of reaction," contradicts Fritz, "most transport systems are standardized. Containers, pallet systems and packaging are interchangeable. Standardization provides us as shippers with favorable prices and the choice among many. But not only the modes of transport are standardized. The procedures are the same. Let's look at transport, storage and handling, up to shift systems and working time regulations. If it were otherwise, nobody would know what's going on anymore."

"You only have to consider one thing", now it's Larissa's turn again, "our products are created beyond the standard. Not only these, but also our projects are unique. The elimination of bottlenecks is usually achieved by special solutions or bypasses. And just not by swapping the provider. The latter, by the way, justifies plan B or C. Otherwise, you would simply have to copy plan A. In our case it means that individuality and responsiveness become the standard. Certainly, many of the classic organizations in logistics reach their limits here. In the worst case, they are not prepared for it at all. You can see it, if they attempt to press the individual product or project into standards".

For Larissa is this the next conflict of goals. She asks: "Why should we abandon standards and give up responsiveness in the first step? I see the", the pen squeaks in the direction, "efficiency as an indicator. The latter stands equally for time saving, economy, cost-benefit ratio and the rational use of scarce resources. For each project task, it is necessary to answer the question: How far the effort for standardization should be driven and how far the pendulum swings in the direction of responsiveness.

As I said, the focus is on our logistics concept for our project. No more and no less," she emphasizes, "certainly, everyone is tempted to generalize. This usually distracts from the concrete solution. Our mission is not to save the world," Warns Larissa.

"That means", asks the student, "we align no longer everything in the construction necessarily to the standard container dimensions, but only where it is efficient for the project, right?"

"We don't use containers here anyway, we pack everything into boxes", Fritz grumbles in between.

"Which always has been made anew for the pleasure of the packer," adds Larissa snappishly, "how long have you actually known each other?

"Okay, that means," Ethan interjects quickly, "that we create with the engineering a specification for the packaging. It oscillates between standardization and reaction. The Indicator is efficiency. This means, for example, that in case of recurring components which do not fit optimally into the container, other reusable packaging will also be used, right?

Eckard immediately starts thinking about the beautiful Christmas presents which her packer donates for her annual raffle. He sees the table half-empty before him.

"This is to be discussed with Peter. Strategic decisions are the matter of the management," he says.

Hit thinks Larissa. Move to the higher level instead of agreement. That's the crux of the matter. Unfortunately, this is the end of the topic for the moment.

They move on to the next question and the eternal dilemma between centralized and decentralized. A common example is the question: central warehouse or not. The classic conflicts of objectives lie between high availability in the vicinity of widely distributed customers, minimum stock levels and optimum use of storage space. For their project they are all contradictory. There is little time in a project for warehouse or inventory optimization. The responsibility for the stocks as well as the transfer of costs and risks changes from contract to contract. The warehouse serves solely to bridge time in the project. If the stocks are deposited centrally or decentral is irrelevant. It is important to track the stocks. Everyone in the meeting room agrees with this analysis.

The discussion on the corrective takes longer. Efficiency, response and standardization are possible. In the end they agree on standardization as a control variable. They focus on the tracking of stocks. The goal is to standardize inventory management as a procedure in the project. Regardless of who is the respective person entitled for the inventory. It is irrelevant where and how many storage locations and warehouses are in the system. In most cases the number is higher than expected anyway. It is imperative that stocks are transparent.

The sales manager had not yet said a word. Well, just listen explained Peter. Nevertheless, he does not feel completely comfortable in his skin. He's a salesman with heart and soul. If there's nothing to say, he suffers like a fish out of water. The arguments which he heard are all understandable to him. The few allegations do not allow any contradiction. Besides, if he would comment anything, his ignorance would have come out.

Older projects are forcing their way into his memory and causing him a queasy concern. He is convinced that he makes strategic and operational decisions on logistics far too often. It's so easy when the customer says and before the deal is closed: " You deliver free at destination for the price ". His "Yes, no problem", comes out like a shot sometimes. Without better knowledge, as he now realizes. His decisions are made without any knowledge of logistics. It feels a little giddy to him. Rarely he has thought about logistics in this depth. It becomes clearer to him that it is too late for an abrupt change in strategy. Not only for the current project, but for the many projects they already have in the pipeline. Is a smooth transition even possible?

Like rocks in the surf sit Eckard and Fritz on the other side of the table. They embody the robust system. Sometimes they even show a true keeper mentality. They are in the boat just like him and the young colleagues. Fritz takes on a double role, as shipping manager and works council member. They'll pull their strings for sure. Even if other colleagues wish to sail on more comfortable and slower courses.

At the end of the day they arrange another meeting. More time is needed for mutual understanding.

At the next reunion Larissa puts her finger into a wound again. Their topic is the high and heavy transports, which requires permits. The number is not small in their project. Robots and devices are included, as are some cranes.

This time sits Peter in the round. Indeed, the reports from the first meeting showed that the mood had not escalated. It was more like a scan. However, nobody talked about progress. Peter wants to get his own picture now. With an unbiased subject. For this reason, he had asked Larissa to contact the high and heavy transports.

Larissa push ahead:

"Why plan B: Heavy haulage is a visible example. We have often sleepless nights without having any influence on the circumstances which decides on top or flop in the project.

Our octagon from the last session will hopefully pass a practical test today. I have prepared a few suggestions, so planning will not anymore be a nightmare.

"What does one thing have to do with the other?" Fritz asks.

"We will test our method with concrete tasks", Larissa replies.

She presents an example: It is about the transport data which are known in the design department at an early stage. In the first step, she would like to work on the dimensions. The robot discussion was hanging in everyone's ears.

"If it is only a few centimeters or if individual parts can be easily dismantled, then these are monetary advantages if dimensions can be reduced. The first target is to avoid heavy transport permits. The prices for transport will fall as a result. We gain time and flexibility," summarizes Larissa.

"In this case, standardization is the corrective between efficiency and response. Do I understand this in the right manner" Ethan asks?

Approving nodding around the table.

"I think such discussions with the construction department are conceivable. Their drawings are even though differed from transport drawings, so we will have to balance between the different images in our minds. However, they know all the sensitive components. I am sure, they will provide us with all the important information that is crucial for vehicles, load securing and anchor points", says Larissa, "the precise summary forms the basis for our Transport, Storage and Handling Manual".

" Of course, I can summarize and researching for the handbook," the student reports to work, "but deciding what is correct and corresponds to the regulations is another thing. I lack the knowledge.

Peter finds more difficult is the discussion with the production. Generally, it´s creates resistance if they will dismantle components that have already been assembled for testing and quality control. After that follows the same on the construction site backwards. The balance between interest and feasibility must be weighed up. Furthermore, he thinks we need to get used to it that the logisticians now suddenly come forward with their objectives permanently.

They decide to sum up transport costs and installation effort in such cases. Fritz interferes briefly by pointing out the many overtime hours, all of which are voluntary. But in the end, he sees the necessity. Efficiency serves as a corrective between redundancy and reaction. For the first time, they are working the sense of an overall logistical consideration. While Peter is thinking about it. Larissa is already at the next step.

She explains: "At the same time we are looking for haulage contractors with permanent permits: If only the width exceeds the permitted 2.55 meters, there are many providers with permanent permits. These sometimes apply to vehicle widths of up to three, 3.20 or 3.50 meters.

If the individual approval cannot be avoided; the process will usually only start after the transport has been ordered. The acceptance of the order is subject to the approval granted. Until then the ball is in our court. The processing time for exception permission is usually two weeks, sometimes more. If the transport is delayed, for example because the customer does not accept the machines, it is imperative that the permit is extended after its validity has expired".

"Who does that for us," Ethan asks, "the logistics purchasing?"

"Who, Logistics Purchasing? We don't have that. These are the tasks of the project purchaser," Eckard answers slightly wet-heartedly.

"This means that each project purchases logistics decentral", asks the student, "are there no more synergies to be gained centrally?

"Sure," Larissa replies, "if the logistics are organized by a unit. Otherwise, it is the task of the logistics purchaser to eliminate the time traps, as described above, as far as possible. This includes route inspections, sometimes including the statics of bridges and tracks, consultation with the police, railway and authorities along the route. The same applies to the examination of transport alternatives. Permission will certainly not be granted if at least partial water or train connections are possible. Economic reasons do not count."

Larissa adds: "With permission, the small print must be read. This includes conditions such as driving time restrictions at rush hour, during holiday periods or for day trips. The possible accompaniment by the police or expert opinions to secure the load are specified before the start of the journey. Conditions that just leave you out in the rain, if you are not aware of them. In our project we travel a bit by ferry. The parking spaces must be booked firmly."

"That's what the hauler does," Fitz interjects.

Larissa ignores the interjection: "As trivial as it sounds, on the other side of the sea the game starts all over again. In international traffic the respective regulations of each country apply. What is allowed in this country does not count in Great Britain, Scandinavia or anywhere else. Especially different holidays must be taken into account here. Day, night and weekend driving times, if ignored, will bring the project timetable into a tailspin. A stop by the police will create in the best-case waiting times including bills. In the worst-case construction may be stopped. And that's a circumstance which are the carrier rarely knows about, Fritz!"

"Let me summarize, it briefly before we discuss it, Fritz," explains Larissa, "Prevention may seem difficult at first glance, but it is not impossible. The application for authorization is made by the hauler in relation to the chosen vehicle combination and at the place where it is registered. He won't do that until he gets the job.

If we work in the future, as discussed so far, the logistics team in the project will push ahead with the planning. This means: Possible variants are determined in advance with the help of design and production. Depending on the dimensions of the components and the project path, we will check the approval capability of the transport".

"What if we just sell 'ex-works' and have the customer come pick them up," asks the sales manager in between. Let's try to think outside the box. Everyone's looking at him.

"The customer will always associate risks or disturbances with our product and name. In case of a follow-up project, he will charge you for this in the price negotiation. In addition, the transfer of costs and risks on the construction site often reverts to us.

He will have an additional interface in his hands that will have a major impact on our project," Ethan replies.

"And what are we going to do with all these worldviews," Eckard asks, "are they going to help us, or have we always been wrong in the past?

"At the very least, we'll increase our mutual understanding. This allows different perspectives. Which in turn pave the way for new methods," answers Peter, "for example: based on the data of individual trades, we can create a visual dashboard with GPS positioning of the transports. This gives everyone a quick overview about the status of deliveries to the construction site. It also shows what is planned. With this information, the construction site and project manager can control the call-offs as required. The timeliness of the data is of course a critical factor which requires maintenance. The logisticians are the spider in the web for this. Suppliers, transporters and the plants of the parent company name contact persons who provide the information. Accordingly, we connect the existing organizations with new technology."

"GPS data of the vehicles are recorded via a database and the tool will further automated. However, this can only be done on a voluntary basis at present, because we lack the agreements with the suppliers. The tool becomes an overarching system for notification and supports the change from the push to the pull-system," adds Larissa, "I find it´s helpful and it fits what I consider necessary.

"Namely what?" Fritz asks.

"Up to now we have had a single-stage logistics system, which only provides direct delivery to the construction site. This is supplemented by a multi-stage process. This means that nodes are organized for time bridging." Larissa sketches both systems on the flipchart. "With this, we're keeping the construction site safe. The aim is to avoid unplanned and simultaneous deliveries of goods as far as possible. Furthermore, we are creating several options for ourselves, which we use according to need. Option one, it is mounted from the truck as originally thought. We supplement this with a trailer concept. The latter makes it possible to park trailers in the port for up to a week after the ferry has arrived. We have managed to clarify this informally with the supplier's forwarding agent. They did not see the necessity at the beginning because they did not know the project processes. However, you now use this option if necessary. Option two: temporary storage outside of the construction site. This is a multi-stage system with a short on carriage. Virtual.AN becomes the stock keeper, because the costs and risks are transferred from the supplier to them. Depending on the progress of the project, additional warehouses in the port will be used, although they generate a longer on carriage. We have enquired with the companies. A list and the offers of the logistics service providers are available. Our last backstop is storage with suppliers or their subcontractors. That remains to be clarified. There are no dependencies to the other solutions," Larissa explains.

"Basically, we are working on concentrating the flow of goods on fewer logistics service providers. The target is to reduce interfaces and create transparency. Of course, all within the framework of existing contracts, on a voluntary basis and with the ongoing project. Some tools are already being picked up on our behalf. The transports are handled by the forwarder, which is also in charge of the robots. They are also active for the supplier who supplies the platforms and vertical conveyors. If possible, serves our empty transport and lifting equipment as return cargo. From the original 63 logistics service providers, the number is currently reduced by 13, although some have been added in the immediate vicinity.

Finally, we avoid costs and interfaces over this way ", Larissa ends her speech.

"And what's the point of it all?" growls Fritz. "Money, which we do not spend or avoid? That's an old hat for me. It's just not an expense. However, the effort that you do is it already. Nobody will take it from you.

"These are just the opposites, Fritz. You are still waiting until the horse had bolted. Then you have free hand, because nobody asks for the costs anymore, as you yourself say," Larissa answers sniffly, "Prevention, on the other hand, requires constant dialogue. For sure many people don't believe you. Until it happens. They usually ask, "why didn't you say it before?"

Fritz nods reluctantly.

"Furthermore, even small effects count. The transport price from East Germany to the construction site was halved by 10,000 euros. The supplier's transport offer from Nuremberg was reduced by 12,000 euros due to the conversion to ex works. Additional claims of 60,000 euros have been rejected with the help of benchmarks. In my view, this is the effect of transparency. If you go through it continuously, you will become more credible in the future with forecasts and warnings," Larissa now argues in a calmer tone.

"Sure, only part of the logistics costs is transparent at all times. The diversity of opinions is just as great as in soccer. Some classify the logistics costs with a share of eight to 14 percent of total sales. For every 10 million euros of project costs, we are then involved with 800,000 to 1,400,000 euros. Others say that 75 percent of the controllable costs in the company depend on logistics and not on the core business," explains Larissa.

"Those are some steep theories," Eckard says.

"When more than half of the controllable costs in a company depend on logistics and not on the core business, this is a huge lever. And the starting point for our new logistics concept!"

Peter puts the brakes on him, "Even the first question is: If there is a way to do this, the necessary monitoring of the logistics is self-evident. In my opinion, it is also permissible to describe the ideal state. These are first without a question theses or theories.

However, the distance to the here and now shows us which bridges and ways we have to build and to enter."

Little by little even Fritz and Eckard get into the "green field" mode. Fritz still mumbles something about cloud cuckoo-land. Afterwards they jointly sketch out a possible ideal picture: They imagine that a colleague who check the last details of a shipment at his desk, sits in the next moment in his car and drive to the port. Once there, he follows all current logistics processes in the project via his mobile device. He adds additional information via photo, video or voice message. A dashboard shows his colleague the comparison between plan data and actual data. Milestones that run the risk of not being met are marked by a traffic light system. The artificial intelligence helps him to forecast the impact of his new data and information on the project on site.

All information for logistics management are bundled centrally. GPS, Internet and sensor technology collect further data. For each authorized person it becomes visible where in the logistic process the shipments are to be found and in which condition. The system makes also recommendations for the next steps. If it´s happens without an AI support, the task remains solely with logistics management.

The platform displays activities such as customs clearance or required transport materials in detail. By means of map and Gantt display, users have a graphical overview of the position of all elements during the entire process. Component lists can be uploaded and used via the import function. The data are assigned to the respective process steps and components and are continuously updated. Access to all data such as delivery documents, certificates, technical drawings is guaranteed. Important milestones in route planning are marked as gates in the planning process.

All screws, components, elements and machines are scanned for the processes to be planned individually. At the end is their transportation the last step. Even the suitable lifting equipment and transport frames to be supplied can be seen by the colleague at the click of a mouse. Movements of materials and information are displayed as a route, which is displayed as a shipment summarized in a dashboard. Information flows thus become intangible transports. Just like the material flows, are they subjected to the eight "R's" of logistics.

If, for example, routes are changed due to traffic jams, alternatives are determined in advance. In the case of the information flows media breaks are led to traffic jams. The effects on schedules are presented transparently. Sensors can be show in real time how the components are doing. Data mining and machine learning will help that the experience gained and can be used for future projects.

A Situation Room is set up and will be expanded into a virtual project room later. They call the Situation Room Routing Center, because the coordination center takes place here. Like the engine control in a passenger car, the logistics systems in the subprojects are coordinated with each other. The interests of the actors involved, who are in the game, are moderated from here. This includes suppliers, service providers, the own company, the construction site and the customer. The clearing office will also be processed unclear or non-transparent data, incidents and claims. It is possible to include several projects and companies in the sense of a "multi-project management".

The implementation of the Routing Center is conceivable in stages: The first step follows the principle "help yourself". In this phase, the company continues to organize its own logistics. The project company provides the support so that all the trump cards of logistics can be used in the project. In the second phase, they call it DIY - do it yourself will the company sets up an own routing center. The project team shows the partner how is the best way to set up and operate it. The third phase follows the "stronger together" principle. Here controls and organizes the project company the logistics of several projects and companies (multi-project management).

Depending on the wishes and what extent the companies involved include logistics among their core competencies, sub-areas such as shipping, or warehousing will remain within the company. The third phase is a hybrid logistics solution that offers a new, more dynamic solution between in-house and outsourcing.

The "Routing Center" logistics concept provides Virtual.AN an independent, virtual organization. It takes over the logistics management of the Virtual.AN projects. The project company is thus given a new task:

- It controls logistics service providers,
- bundles communication and transport flows,
- ideally uses two to three logistics service providers per function,

- relieves the project participants at all levels from logistics tasks and
- increases process and cost transparency.

The tasks of transport service providers are also changing. In principle, transports are ordered like taxis. Everything before and after that, such as, in the figurative sense, packing the suitcases, getting on and off the bus or picking up colleagues, will be done himself in future.

Furthermore, a new bridge to customers and suppliers is being built and used. In addition to the existing links between the projects, purchasing and management the logistics relationship will be formally created. It is expected to operate more informally and beyond the commercial aspects of the customer relationship. Over this way it serves as a further source of information for the project. The cost, process and quality control of the suppliers, which takes place via performance descriptions, specifications, contracts or construction supervision, is subsequently extended to logistics.

Finally, there are other reasons for this: Up to now, logistics service providers have not been sufficiently evaluated by customers and suppliers. They work more in the background. They are correspondingly difficult to schedule for the project team. At the same time, their efficiency is crucial for a secure supply of the project. Furthermore, often they do not have enough and project-specific information. This is where the cat bites its tail. Then follows: The higher the number of service providers in the project, the more interfaces are created. The risk of information breaches increases, which inevitably has an impact on the project flow. If this has occurred, the exclusions in the transport contracts usually refer to the fact that the project must solve the problem itself. The whole thing will then take into the next "loop".

Taking these factors into account, they continue to work on the new logistics concept of Virtual.AN in the following weeks. They formulate key points, such as flexibility in production. Evaluate the usefulness of market enquiries for calculating their own prices. Achieve a common understanding for make or buy decisions.

Epiloge

After the game is before the game - without dogma to the goal through "Business Sparring Logistics

Well, what now? This plot is moving. As in maritime shipping, it stands for the representation of positions and external influences such as wind and currents. Which ones influence your personal success in the company? How do you keep logistics on course or at least sail in calm waters? In this sense we work according to the motto: prevention before optimization. Cost prevention is direct profit for the company! If is your target, we will analyses your own business processes and set the course so that you can targeting your potential yourself!

Sometimes a partner is necessary for the design. Everybody's just biased. Is stuck in your own attitude. Has rough edges. Besides, clarification is tedious and sometimes painful. In this case, you want a sparring partner who shows what works and what goes wrong.

What didn't work here is, as with the lyrical plot, to describe a general framework of action for modern logistics concepts. History has changed too much for that. I bent it. Sometimes broken and then patched. I was twisting. And sent the protagonists on a previously open circular path. Let's face it, isn't that what the reality is? Isn't that where we all find ourselves? If I had started here in the usual order with the classic table of contents, the plot would have been static. Never would've gotten to where he is now.

We are on fire when it comes to maintaining the accustomed order. At the same time, you see the water and the fears rising, which brings us into swimming. However how do you describe it? What comes closer to reality? Like here with the renunciation of classical structures or as guideline for the logistic senses.

Whatever we call ourselves, whether consultant, planner or trainer. We are sparring partners. In the story Larissa slipped into this role unintentionally. As I said, it wasn't planned. She's as biased as everyone else, because she is just doing her job in the project. Finally, the idea of extending business sparring into the logistics is the result of simply writing on it.

Many people know sparring from boxing. In a training situation fight the partners similarly as in competition. Perhaps therefore is the term so widely used in the business world. It is used for coaches and mentors as well as for trainers who get into a practice situation with the coaches or mentee. Business Sparring is a way to think through and reflect important decisions in the company with an independent partner. The aim is to improve the skills of the actors in the company. The sparring partner is available to prepare new, difficult tasks. The important thing is that the chemistry is right. So that you're on the same wavelength.

In this sense, before you post a job offer for the management and development of your logistics. Why do you not use a manager from your own team? They already have considerable knowledge of in-house logistics. Without this your business would not function. Your team knows your products best and that is decisive. Everything else such as new methods, tactics and strategies in logistics, must be communicated to the next generation of managers via Business Sparring Logistics. Nevertheless, if you work in projects, you are more likely to enter uncharted territory. The objectives differ accordingly.

If you like to strive in the next step, with heart and soul to control and develop all logistical processes in your company: The logistics becomes the linchpin. This is the first step towards Logistics 4.0, which stands for the networking and integration of logistics processes - inside and outside of production plants - up to the control of logistics networks in real time.

If you want to make better friends with your logistics in this sense? Our Business Sparring offers the possibilities for this. We proceed as in a workshop talk: The focus is on direct and informal exchange with you and your colleagues. Take the first step today and try out our new workshop configurator on our website https://logistik-service-agentur.com/wissen-teilen/

Like a catering service for the event, you are invited to plan your menu here for your own in-house workshop discussion. Every new menu, like its recipe, is a speculation for the respective taste. If there will be several courses, it is recommended that they fit together. We will gladly give you the appropriate tips. In line with our plot we deliver fiery, exotic, sweet and sour impulses.

How much time do you take depends on how much knowledge your employees "eat" and how the "small talk" succeeds in trying things out. The aim, as in cooking school or a team academy is for you to take home as many tips and suggestions as possible for your (working) day-to-day life.

As an exotic starter, we propose abstract comparisons. For example: What does an open-air concert have to do with the erection of wind turbines? Logistics is like fast food. It's almost always the same. Projects, on the other hand, are unparalleled, just like a good wine. In this sense we sort terms and uncover contradictions. Compare recipes and see what the others do. We look for the common denominator for your logistics in the project and try a quick check.

It continues like "Halloween" sweet or sour. Logistics works when nobody notices anything. If so, the logistics taste like a well-mixed cocktail! If not, it may be due to cheap ingredients. Once the logistical baton has fallen the pressure is quickly felt in the head. How do the ingredients of the logistics work best so that sweet and sour complement each other? How do forwarder and project become a couple, like cook and waiter; who does what? How do project managers and logistics managers find a common line? In this segment we are preparing the "Mise en Place".

The next course may become fiery in the finish: How compatible are the methods of project and logistics management. The variations are as numerous as finger food. Their recipes generate terms like "Agile", "Six Sigma", "Scrum" or "Critical Chain". The same applies to logistics. There are "Eight R`s",

"Just in Time", "Just in Sequence", "Pull-" and "Push", "Hub and Spoke", "Relay Stick" and much more. How does it all fit together? Which combination best serves which purpose.

The main course is in line with the trend: How ready are digital instruments for use in projects and logistics? Digitization is like a "smoothie": it may be healthy, but you often don't know what's in it and how it gets to you. In the project it is better if it is good for the project. Nobody will afford experiments. We show how to approach the requirements and evaluate use cases. We test the maturity of digital thoughts on the levels of processes, networking and technology.

Just like classic plain cooking, they are always returning to the menu: the conflicting goals. Everyone is caught up in this dichotomy and not only in logistics. If you detect them early they will not boil up and will not come into focus. We show the classic conflicts and try a new method of determining the right core temperature for you. So that the logistics succeeds according to your taste from "rare" to "well done".

In the end, the question hovers over the whole thing again and again: aperitif or digestif; which view of logistics achieves the greatest benefit? We cannot promise an explosion of taste; the subject is indeed too dry for that. But to make sure that, like peeling an onion, the perspectives do not blur. We take new ones and show you how to find out your benefits. With an inventory for your project we see what it already has in stock. We read recipes or contracts - logistically between the lines - and design the departure with first sketches. We derive the ingredients for your logistics concept from the project plans.

Finally, Larissa, Peter and Ethan look back and formulate five topics for which they would like to see "Business Sparring Logistics". "It's up to you to add others," Peter calls out to the group:

They call the first topic area: "Start up - managing logistics": Not only in the business plan, but also in the project plan, one usually reads about logistics between the lines. "Business Sparring Logistics" makes sure that no headlines arise from this. It questions whether and how the plans are compatible with the logistics world. Many strategy issues and "make-or-buy" decisions stand in the way of this.

The second subject area follows from this. They described it with: Improve balance sheet, reduce inventories, cut costs. Only the value of goods appears as the logistics key figure inventory in the balance sheet. Depending on how you look at it, there are further items on logistics costs. For some, these are just the transport costs, others have 300 other cost items on the slip of paper. Where these stands are to be worked out via "Business Sparring Logistics". After that turns the set screws in visible.

The third topic area already has one goal in mind: to enrich Supply Chain Management and make logistics profitable. Far more than half of the controllable costs in the supply chain of companies depend on logistics, not on the core business. If that applies to you as well, it is a huge lever. This is how Peter sums up the guiding principle. "Business Sparring Logistics" starts here, especially since this knowledge is possibly new territory for other departments such as sales, purchasing and construction.

Time and again, one ends up with the topic of organizational development. Logistics affects all areas of the company. She is a duty. Nothing works without them. The fourth field is at the first glance a classic for "Business Sparring Logistics". It shows how logistics can save time, simplify work and improve product availability.

In the end, the topic from the beginning is found again: How to make project and logistics management as compatible as possible. Logistics repeats itself, projects are unique. This is the first conflict of objectives in which a project runs the risk of falling under the wheels of logistics. More will follow. The logistical baton principle almost always sprints along the critical path in a project. That's bound to cause trouble. How project and logistics managers find a common line, "Business Sparring Logistics" provides the impetus.

In this sense, after the game is before the game.